Yearbook

Indian Poetry in English
2023

Yearbook

Indian Poetry in English
2023

Editors
SUKRITA PAUL KUMAR
VINITA AGRAWAL

Pippa Rann
books & media

Pippa Rann
books & media

An imprint of
Salt Desert Media Group Limited,
7 Mulgrave Chambers, 26 Mulgrave Rd,
Sutton SM2 6LE, England, UK.
Email: publisher@pipparannbooks.com
Website: www.pipparannbooks.com

First published by Pippa Rann Books & Media, U.K.
ISBN 978-1-913738-12-9

Printed and bound at Replika Press Pvt. Ltd.

Dedicated to the symphony
of diverse voices in Indian poetry

CONTENTS

Editors:

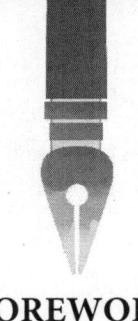

FOREWORD

The extraordinarily warm reception of the first three volumes of the Yearbook, tremendously boosted our morale as Editors, for the continuation of the Yearbook project into this fourth volume in the series. We are happy to announce that the Yearbook of Indian poetry in English will henceforth be published by Pippa Rann Books, UK, produced with the gracious support of Prabhu Guptara, the publisher. With this, we hope to widen its readership to the international arena. We are indeed thankful to Hawakal Publishers, New Delhi, for supporting the concept and publishing the initial three Yearbooks.

As always, this year too, the submissions for the Yearbook, were overwhelmingly abundant. We received over 700 poems this year. For one, this is a sign that poetry in English in India and by Indians abroad is being written with great enthusiasm and plenty of aspirational fervour. A striving to excel as much in creative expression as in content, can be amply seen in the poems submitted. The very first poem included in this year's edition articulates the ardent compulsion of the poet to write in this simple line *"...all I can worry about these days, are things that remain unsaid."* Is there then a compelling need in a poet to locate what "remains unsaid"? Does the poet dive adventurously into the deep ocean to hunt for an oyster with rare pearls? Quality poems picked up for the Yearbook are like a treasure trove built with utmost care and without prejudice. The process of selection remains anonymous each year through a different composition of the Review Committee every year, comprising both young and old poets. We are grateful to Imtiaz Dharkar, Vivek

Narayanan, Mani Rao and Madhu Raghavendra to have accepted to be on the committee and spare their time and efforts to help us choose the best poems from amongst the 200 long-listed poems sent to them from the submissions this year.

Selected from poems published in the year 2023 (January to December), and then having gone through a process of a rigorous sifting of quality poems, what is offered to the reader, is a collection of poems that deserves to be showcased for the contemporary reader and archived for posterity. With several independent niche publishers for Indian poetry in English along with different online social media handles for projection of poetry, there seems to be a surge of poetry in our times. In such a scenario there is a strong possibility of overlooking good poetry that might just slip into the oblivion for the sheer lack of promotion or recognition. The Yearbook is consciously planned towards presenting objectively sifted poetry that can set aesthetic pointers on the one hand and also put on record the shifts in content year by year. The Yearbook produced during the pandemic times showed how the poetic sensibility was grappling with disease, death, massive migration of the poor from the cities to their rural homes, economic stress and the desperation in the face of a collapse of resources taken so much for granted earlier. The following two Yearbooks published in 2022 and 2023 changed in tone and tenor. The poems captured a mood of reflection and resolution. Rather than cynicism and a sardonic portrayal of the destiny of humankind, there seemed to be a conscious effort to confront the need to change the norms of living and development. A greater focus on climate change, environmental degradation, gender equation and the need to build stronger relationships is exhibited in poetry.

The Beacon Light section of the Yearbook 2023 highlights the poem "Another Need" by the illustrious, veteran poet Bibhu Padhi. This is followed by a new section titled Commemoration dedicated to Nissim Ezekiel. His centennial year of birth is to be celebrated in the current year 2024. Thanks to his daughter Kavita, the section carries his poem "The Second Candle" written in his own hand.

This year, one of the distinctive features in the selected poems turns out to be that of many poets unravelling their connection with their mothers or fathers – overtly or covertly – either lingering in memory after their passing or staying alive in the heart through their skills in the kitchen. And then there were those searing lines in the poems stemming from a space of deeply disturbing incidents - *Last year, when my father let in the darkest night/ mum vowed to eat all 12 purnima moons/ so their lights would spill out of her/ in the shape of little fairies/ purple and green.* Also there's the absolutely graphic tribute to what a 'father' represents - *"they wait on scooters/at right angles to the sun/measuring the slowness of/the summer heat/Against the rapidly approaching bright/future they wish upon their sons."*

Running parallel to these poems are poems that revolve around grandparents – grandmas and grandpas. Through different poetic narratives they convey the wholesome, rounded roles that the older generation has played in shaping the thought processes and personalities of the younger generation. Several poems are, understandably, themed around women too; from references to their shimmering Kanjeevarams, status of their hairdos, their art of cooking, their folding piles of clothes to feeling inconsequential as a housewife, and on the other hand is the sexual exploitation of women. Interestingly there is also an unusual tactical use of the word 'woman' as a verb – *"to woman is to witness/changes in set semantics/the word guilt, for instance"*

One of the concerns to be found in many a poem is that of identity which projects itself through the voicing of angst of an exile strangely in one's own homeland. The poet's attention is pulled towards the local as much as global contexts. There is the feel of a specific angst of the contemporary times although there are also anxieties regarding the perennial existential predicament of humankind. That is why perhaps the artist/poets keep struggling to find the right voice and an appropriate form to express themselves.

It may be pointed out here that the current Yearbook carries a diversity of forms of poetry. From haibun to haiku, ghazals to concrete poems, our poets have been experimenting with form with a serious engagement. Ghazals included here are embellished with words from the original Urdu or Hindi, thus lending a layer of authenticity and richness to the verses. The ghazals in this year's edition are particularly poignant and interestingly, on varied themes as well. In free verses too there are some lines boldly included in the original Tamil, Telugu or Malayalam languages, some even in their original script, others in anglophone phonetics proving without doubt that this is poetry unmistakably from India. Poetry here seems to be embracing all four directions of our land, not to forget the beautiful north-east. Some poems are dedicated to the recent unrest in Manipur by poets living in other parts of the country. Alongside is the exquisite poetry written by poets from within the north-eastern regions. The unpretentious expression about nature, rivers and trees and native culture is particularly remarkable – *"I've learned to live with the land/not from the land, and sometimes/the mountain sings back to me."* It is heartening that included here are several pertinent poems on environment and ecology – *"If trees are my ancestors/then all elements on the earth/are proofs of my history."* Forceful, impactful and powerful poems. The degenerative condition of nature around us is prodding poets to take up these themes with an urgency as though in a desperate bid for corrective measures.

Whatever be the form or content of the poems in the Yearbook, each poem possesses a universal and comprehensive appeal even though it emerges from the personal space of the poet. That is the beauty of putting together an anthology like this; showcasing poems born from the unique experiences of the poet but being read and understood by readers globally due to their universal appeal. The personal turns relevant, the distinctive turns intimate and the particular turns characteristic of the general human being.

As editors we have been also very attentive to the issue of the use of language by the poets writing in English in these times. Gradually Indian poetry in English seems to have come of age and the carpet is laid out for the demonstration of both, the variety of styles as well as plurality of concerns, being brought to light for the world to delve into our inner cartography. What is crucial is to also acknowledge the 'owning'of English language here, the process that was discussed by the eminent writer Raja Rao in his Preface to *Kanthapura* (1938): "We are all instinctively bilingual, many of us writing in our own language and in English. We cannot write like the English. We should not. We can write only as Indians…Our method of expression therefore has to be a dialect which will some day prove to be as distinctive and colourful as the Irish or the American." Well, Raja Rao's prophesy has come true. Most of the poems collected in the four volumes of the Yearbooks amply reflect that in the tonal quality, idiom as well as rhythms, they reflect a bilingual sensibility. Written in English, they are well rooted in the culture they emerge from, be it Punjabi, Malayalam or any other Indian language. There is evidence of the courage of retaining the untranslatable words or the idioms in the poems written in the original English.

The four volumes of the Yearbook are a wake-up call to critics and scholars: these Yearbooks offer more than adequate selected Indian poetry of recent times, for them to formulate a critical treatise on the subject; in addition the sense of tradition growing in contemporary poetry calls for serious attention. The body of creative work showcased in the Yearbook now seeks suitable theoretical tools to examine this poetry critically.

We would like to end with a celebratory note - a warm toast of good cheer and admiration for the vast canvas of Indian poetry in English. We feel blessed and honoured to continue this project of compiling poems into a compendium year after year. Thank you fellow poets for affording us the privilege of reading your beautiful work. We would also like to thank our readers for their interest in and support of the Yearbook across the passage of time. Thank you everyone involved in the making of this volume.

Sukrita and Vinita

June 2024

ABHISHEK ANICCA
The Curse of Hephaestus

I wrote a song for a withering flower on the balcony, without knowing what beauty is.
A man stood inside the mirror in my room, measuring corners of fat on my chest.
We played hopscotch; you said I could use both legs if one of them was dead.
Love murmured confessions, you were the rhythm, I was a song, in spring.
A video playlist discovered me on the internet, forcing me to practice stoicism.
I met three hundred people online pretending to be a Nobody under Emily's watch.
My friend realized not everyone uses the sound of tch every time they meet a cripple.
News. The literary criticism of my legs wrote a poem, ranting about the winter weather.
I have deleted thirteen long slow-motion videos that I had shot from my hospital bed.
A person on a fetish site said if I was the last man alive, they would choose death.
Between American and British English, I prefer the beauty of the word unmade.
You say Umami, I feel guilty of watching food videos without losing any weight.
The ongoing research exploring the effect of light on my pee has kept me busy.
I often wonder what eulogy you will write for me now that we live in different cities.
A dog waits to adopt me, a cat awaits my betrayal, a rat sleeps peacefully in my room.
The world is ending, and all I can worry about these days, are things that remain unsaid.

Published in NO NIIN, *Issue 20, Vol. 3, October 2023.*

ADITI GARG

Inconsequential Life of a Half-housewife

how do you look away
from girls in skirts belts turned
over at the top to be shorter
knees stark like pebbles
shirts gently pulled out
at the waist to let the breast
defy catholic school norms
the sway of the haughty ponytail
the walk intoxicating
cultured ethos of upbringing neglected
bottling up a run to the river of youth
snatching the bends and curves
awaited forever
waiting
waiting
waiting
to move so toes trouble breath
to be delicious

Published in hākārā, *an online bilingual journal in English and Marathi, 28.12.2023*

AFTAB YUSUF SHAIKH
Devasthan

When gypsy tribes move
From camp to camp,
What they are looking for is blessings, shelter and
A rotten piece of bread,

When rotten souls move around,
They look for hungry eyes and flat stomachs of fathers
With flat eyes, flat destinies.

But one certain day, a week actually,
Some people used a palm of sacred water to douse a forest fire,
How do I say it, what they did!
A small child for their desires!

A flower plucked and crushed
And turned to paste, a flower yet to
Even gain fragrance. And first time
Ever a flower was taken, to the temple but not for
any god, or god-like
Stone. But for the devil within.

The god within, if there was one,
Covered its eyes with its palms
And walked out of the temple
Helplessly.

First published in Usawa Literary Review, *May 17, 2023*

AJAY KUMAR

my father decides to wait but forgets to decide

i see my mother coil the air around her
finger talking on the phone. i remember
the knot in the spiral cord of the landline
as we plucked it out and dusted it off
when we moved out of the old house.

i remember my father filling out forms at
the BSNL office for the return of the now
small amount they'd then paid as deposit
when they first got connection a decade ago.
i remember thinking my father was miserly.

i remember the torn ten rupee note he'd saved
to cellotape later. i remember he'd known misery
working for the building he stayed in to be allowed
to stay on while he looked for some real work.
i hear my mother tell my father on the phone to stop
waiting for the bus and to just take an auto instead.

on my way to the cybercafé to play counterstrike
on LAN i used to see words scrawled on the glass
of the phone booth that the dew was too weak
to wet and erase knowing whoever wrote it
must've run out of coins, out of time, of places
to fiddle with, but not out of words to touch upon.

i remember my parents queued outside the phone
booth on halfprice sundays to call back home. i don't
know if i was already there or only going to be.
i remember how no one accepted the cellotaped note.
i know the deposit never came. my father still waits.

Published in The Chakkar, *June 2023*

AKSHADA SHROTRYIA
Measurements

ages ago when they decided my grandmother had reached a
      marriageable age
my great-grandmother taught her the art of cooking

and she dared to ask the question that has boggled mankind
ever since The Creation
ever since Brahma carved the universe
ever since Allah shaped Adam from dust –

ekchutkinamakkitnahotahai?

and my great-grandmother turned to meet –
amidst the crackling of jeera in hot ghee –
a pair of innocent and clueless 12-year-old eyes.

she held the side of my grandmother's face softly
smiled the deepest of smiles and said

tumkhudsamajhjaogi.

~~~

years ago when they decided all their kids should know the art of
      cooking –
for it was a basic need if you wanted to make a living in the city away
      from the small town –
my mother decided she needed to learn it too
and she dared to ask the question that still continues to baffle
      mankind –
maa, ekchutkinamakkitnahotahai?

to which my grandmother lovingly replied
tumkhudsamajhjaogi.

~~~

months ago when i decided to learn the art of cooking –
i asked my mother to teach me some basics

and as you well know by now,
i too, dared to ask the question that has remained a serious mystery to
      mankind all over the planet –

mummy, ekchutkinamakkitnahotahai?

and my mother laughed

batao na?

she replied

tum khud samajh jaogi.
samay sab sikha dega.

Published in The Punch Magazine, *4th March, 2023*

AMIT SHANKAR SAHA
Judah

What if April is the cruellest month,
like you said quoting the poet?
How cruel can it be?

Maybe this month a country
will be wiped out like Judah
when the Babylonians came.

Maybe the tragedy will not be
the decimation of a kingdom
but the separation of two people.

If love is the victim,
exile is the cruelty.
How many Aprils you need?

Why blame a month? Just
a day, a moment is enough
to be the cruellest?

Maybe memory is Babylon,
desire a dead land with dull roots,
lilacs my fingers,

your hand the spring rain.
Maybe April is the cruellest month
if you are Russia and I Ukraine.

Published in Saaranga Magazine, *1st June 2023*

AMLANJYOTI GOSWAMI
Silk

Fragrant Kanjeevaram, shimmering Benarsi, slippery Dhakai.
Our stolen eyes meet half-way in the past.

Silk once ran down our lives
Our breath one, the warp and weave

Unravelling with the morning sun.
But here you are, rolling out miles

Of fresh green muslin, white draping jasmine.
Salty guava, trinkets of fire, a flowing river

To a new customer, as you murmur
One arc to another, like a new border.

And I hold cloth between thumb and forefinger,
Smell starch, pause between breath

Between glittering walls, asking silk
To show the way again.

Where will the sari fall – your side or mine?
Where will our roads lead this time?

Published in The Passionfruit Review, *April 2023*

ANANNYA NATH
my mother's dreams

my mother's dreams are
neon skies
peppered with pounded rice
and three different courses at ten.
they are jargons used in a French cook book;
the betel nuts tied to her *sador's aasol*
breaking under the nut-cracker's weight-
discarded pomegranate seeds.
my mother's dreams are dinner table accusations
of "where's the salt?"
of "did you learn nothing at your mother's house?"
of "this, again?"
my mother's dreams are
overcooked meals;
the one time she left the stove on
and never returned-
a kitchen on fire;
charred wishes,
burnt food.

Published in Gulmohur Quarterly, *June 2023.*

ANIL PETWAL
Learning on Stranger Shores

Teach yourself
By looking at a singular thing of magic each day
Said grandfather.

So I visited the river each day
Its little waves bred of the fierce winds
And the whirlpools where the water swirled
Were meant to be my wordless guides.

Like a hermit on probation
I waited for epiphanies
That came some days as little birds
Leapt at the moats of the pouring sun
Imitating Icarus in an alternate universe.

Then there were days when old men on boats
Cast their fishing nets
Heedless of the brewing storms
Willing to brave the elements
Just for a little catch.

And one noon as teenage swimmers
Emerged from the raging waters
Like conquistadors having deflated a common foe
I saw my long abandoned self in their fearless walk.

With scenes like these the days flashed past
Each sight a baton to a new truth
Swirling, leaping, coming in to its own
Amid a lapping of water against stone.

Published in The Hooghly Review, *Issue 2, 15/10/23*

ANJU KISHORE
Kaleidoscope

I decide to watch a Tamizh movie at the local *kotaai*, a rough
structure made of thatched mud that runs shows of not so
new releases. My mother, fearing the God-knows-what kind
of people a city-bred adolescent might encounter there, is
with me. We get our tickets from a *banian* and *lungi* clad
man inside a faded tin enclosure. A *beedi* quivers at his dark
lips when he drawls that he has no change.

We duck into the cinema theatre. As mother had warned,
most of it has only the bare ground as seating. A few chairs
dot the wall at the far end. We go for them but end up
grabbing each other in alarm. Both chairs stand on about
three-and-a-half legs. The rest that look only slightly better
are occupied. We stare at the floor with rows of oiled heads,
resplendent in the semi darkness with all kinds of flowers.
Mother sighs and we lower ourselves on the sand among the
glitter of colourful saris. The ladies pause to look at us but
carry on with their high-pitched banter till the show begins.
An hour or so into the movie, somebody settles down quietly
into the dark beside me.

All too soon, the little door is thrown open to a burst of
sunshine and a wave of gabble. Next to me, a one-eyed street
dog licks my dusty fingers and presses closer.

sip of a river
the taste of everything
in its path

Published in haiku KATHA *Issue 17, Mar 2023*

ANUSHRI NANAVATI
Migratory Bird

Love me with the backbones of a hundred Decembers,
between the ridged boughs of our naked sentrees;
Love me with the tremors of frigid catalepsy,
while winter anapests crawl into our bones.
Love me with the frailty of January dreams,
wear me like a skin.
I flitted thrushes underneath your lids,
flight whickered between your lashes.
Your feathers fluttered down my cheek:
you moulted mid-flight.
They say you were a migratory bird,
that given time you would return,
fly back to me, your winter home,
That like Scheherazade, your plumage
would nightly flicker tales,
nestled between my breasts:
But you'd always fly away.
Love me with the frostlings of February whims,
between the whispers of the wind.
Love me with the flotsam of muslin hypothermia,
While arctic tenderness descends upon our brow.
Love me with the futility of holding March at bay,
wrap me in your wings, before you fly away.

Published in Birds, Bones, & Melancholia: Musings and Mutterings, *Resource Publications, an imprint of Wipf and Stock Publishers, August 6, 2023*

ARJUN RAJENDRAN
The Fridge

Look, no more chamadumpas,
kovakais or obese baingans.
Just artisanal pork, bhoot
jolokia and kebabs: no more
need to lie about the red meat.

Your head, Ma, conceals well
among the cabbages. When
I peeled open your eye-lid
three days from the mortuary,
as you lay before the oven

bathed, in a currant black gown,
your sister slapped my wrist.
But it was too late: I'd already
seen. The retina, like curd you'd
half-eaten with avakaya pickle,

then stored away un-lidded
for maggots: such *culture*.
No more broken coconuts,
withered jasmine or marigold.
The snake gourd is not for God.

Above the tray empty of insulin
 needles, eggs not devilled.
The pet mongoose, (when
I was nine?) munching squid
when you opened the door

Now sits comfortably atop
the beer and wine bottles,
enjoying sushi with a chopstick.
My memory, unlike supermarket
vegetables, isn't lacking in flavour.

Published in Usawa Literary Review, *Issue 9, June 2023*

ARUN PARIA
The Cobra Eaters

Hanoi, 2022

When it's cut from the body
with one chop,
in Hang Ha Noi restaurant,
the king cobra's
severed head yawns.
In the death dream, the fangs come
out to bite, then hide
inside the sleeping jaws.
The headless body
leaps
high from the metal pan,
gets tangled
with the wiggling tail.
Minutes later, it's skinned,
slit with kitchen
knife, dripping blood
into a plastic cup.

It's still alive. In a way
we're alive when we recuse
the body
to sleep, tuck
our fangs in
in a helpless yawn,
poison hid
in the nook of the heart.
The sleeping torsos jerk

at the thud of a chop,
thump the ground
with a fuming tail:
when we cobra eaters crawl
in the hollow
of the night
slowly serpentine
between dream and death.

Published in Heartwood Literary Magazine, *Issue 15, Spring 2023*

ATHIRA UNNI
Postcard from England

We have crossed the sea now to live in
the coloniser's island. Labels of heaven,
hell, purgatory: irrelevant in a fresh plump
marriage. Uneventful days. I see a thistle
roll across the savage, somnolent moors.

At a distance, an octopus church stands
under clouds like grey puffy sugar candy.
In the gloom of waiting next to graves,
it stretches its tentacles along the streets.
The berried trees and driveways stir

and a bright red post-van disappears.
I think of my grandfather, his stamps,
the retired postmaster of his village
stretched out on his odorous old bed.
An old woman sneezes, keeps walking.

English has its poised lilts that scorn me.
Fish and chips and curry and baked beans
become recipes. My dowdy oven knows some
embarrassing secrets of burnt Sunday roasts.
Tickets booked. But we never go back home.

Trains arrive, depart. The sea is home-turf.
Its rules are simple: wave hello, goodbye.
It frames all: the sun, a boat, arrival, our life.
At a castle by the sea, a little boy runs, laughs
and falls to his knees, the rocks still and wise.

Published in Channel Magazine, *Issue 8, Summer 2023.*

ATREYEE MAJUMDER
Lilac

In the name of the cowherd god,
You turned pink at the turn of the clock.
When cattle walk home,
I take my phone out to square you out onto an IG story.
This story is interrupted
time and time again
by tentacles of this ugly city -
people's bobbing heads, and truck headlights.
Bangalore grows into Eternity
And my taxi ride never ends.
I square and square your lavender
But it spills out of my frame.
IG stories be damned!
Damn you, lilac piece of sky, I say,
You belong in my smartphone
You belong in my pink cocktail
You belong in my colourless heart -
I need to grab you like sand-granules in my five fingers.
This ugly city shields you from private ownership.
The cowherd sky refuses my phone, my wallet, my finger, my heart.

Published in RIC Journal, 17 *February 2023.*

BABITHA MARINA JUSTIN
The New Word We Learned

The first time Prof. Thomas taught us
anachronism in *Dr. Faustus*,
we tittered, jangled our bangles
and pleated our pallus
with our shy, sweaty palms.
ആനin Malayalam is an elephant,

in our arrogant prattle of the young
ക്രോണി was madness. We laughed at
the 'madelephant 'flung at our face.

Everything tickled us, the handsome professor
cracked a joke to distract the class,
we had read them in
BobanumMollyum comic strips.

He glanced at us like lightning,
chewed his moustache and spelled
'necromancy'. Nothing to do with
either neck or romance, he hissed.
That zipped us up with a double-edged stab.

Years later, I met Prof. Thomas,
arthritic and obese. He could no longer
teach, but he lingered like an anachronism,
senility drooling from his mouth corners,
in a room full of freshly washed grand-children.

My neck ached for the kiss
of the new words we learned.

Published in Forty Five Shades of Brown, *Poetrywala 2023*

BARNALI RAY SHUKLA
New Shores

That hourglass is not looking to stand still
to tell the time to a world that won't listen

it has secrets in the grains of sand that
murmurs of a shy crab, rays that sing

of a watery sun, light on edge of a shoal
lost under a lighthouse, foghorn like mom

calling for lunch, waiting to trace
a family united by grief but nothing

on their lips
save stories

of mini meals, with fingers of
sunshine, gentle on kelps

swaying to messages in bottles
meant for others, they long for

good fathers like seahorses
putting their babies back to sleep, hoping

                                    they learn to dream...

Published in The Hooghly Review, *Edition 2, October 2023*

BASUDHARA ROY
Woman at Twilight

At the day's end
the woman
has nothing in her hands.

Everything on it
has been quietened to satisfaction,
to rise tomorrow in mutiny again.

She doesn't know
how many times this day
she has put her feet and fingers to use.

She forgets
how many laws she has upheld or
how many goodbyes she has said.

She is aware only
of having walked all day
and of not having covered an inch.

Ask her weary body or uncombed mind
what arrival means
and her eyes will startle you out of answers.

In her potholed being,
aches resolutely linger in pockets
like rainwater.

Come, find her at twilight
rinsing her day
of whatever it has drunk.

Published on Live Wire, The Wire *15th March, 2023*

BENI SUMER YANTHAN
Please Do Not Touch
(A poem on the repatriation of Naga ancestral human remains from the Pitt Rivers Museum, Oxford)

Across these crooked mountains where the land curtsies to the rivers
And the raw timbres of tattered history meanders into the songs
Of my forefather and my foremother –
Songs I now sing with broken syllables and mismatched tones,
I am comforted by the ghosts that live in them
Ghosts that wake upon such an invocation
Whose lives have previously leaked out of the crevices of these songs
And have become transmuted into objectionable topics of study one
      holds
Between their fingers as they discuss anthropological indiscretions
Overproduced in seminar halls and monetised by museums.
They say they wish to return to their land where myths are contained
Not in twisted tongues or caged in glass boxes stained with the
      interdiction –
"Please do not touch",
Or on labels where a child's game lie paralysed in description,
Where people come and gawk and say, this is spectacular!
But to return home where people walk and move with the earth,
where the water of the forest nurses the wounds of the heart
where touch has no mediator
and the truth has no dialect.

My friend, tell me, how can you and I tell them that this
is just another dream that one keeps to oneself?

Published in The Bangalore Review, *May 2023*

40

BHASWATI GHOSH
Wrapping Love

At first it was about bending geometry.
Folding a square into a triangle and turning
that into a circle wrapping your head.
You could have been a Russian or Ukrainian
peasant woman working hard in a field.
In reality, you were only a school girl
braving a north Indian winter.

The head, a sphere spawning ever new worlds.
The head, also the seat of wit
and silken hair, treasures to protect.
Women at war and in worship,
school girls in Kabul and Delhi,
desert belles in Kutch, we all wear it.

Every Sunday, my Nigerian neighbour's head
is the prettiest in the entire neighbourhood.
Geles of Nile blue and Grand Canyon vermilion,
Amazon green and canary yellow burst upon
her head like bird nests and ocean beds.

Love is what wraps you, I was told.
But love is also what you can wrap.
A scarf. A wimple. A hennin. A hijab. A dupatta.

First published in The Bombay Literary Magazine, *August 2023*

BINU KARUNAKARAN
Pattanam

in the summer, the roots // in the rains, stones
of the strychnine tree went // agate, amethyst,
deep into the earth // beryl and quartz,
full of bitterness past // garnet and carnelian
the bones of the dead // rose up from the depths
and clasped the cool, lustrous // like memories of lost love,
pearls from a broken anklet // played hide and seek
mistaking the seeping light // with seeds ousted from
for spring water // twisted pods of coral trees.

Published in Muse India e-journal, *Issue 111 Sep-Oct 2023.*

CAROL D'SOUZA
History

That sail on the horizon was always
going to be a shroud, O good people
The emperor in a further coup
managed to trade his clothes

Follow the Ms
Maluku, Manchester, Massachusetts
Muting mechanistic metaphysics
More and more and more

The high of the poppy
strained into the tea
with a side of spices

What the body knew escaped
Descartes. Like Linnaeus after him
Binary binomial brothers
building the blocks

MEANING meaning more than money
Magic no longer doing the trick

Power is in the pipelines now
but the patterns peek
through the palimpsest

Portents

with thanks to Amitav Ghosh

Published in EKL Review *Issue 9, April 2023*

CHAITALI SENGUPTA
Stories that Came Before Me

My mother died a refugee.

Walking backwards would take her back,
she always thought.
Take her back from where she left. To the
moment before she fled.

Back to her village, near the Euphrates,
in the land of
palm trees and sun. But Time has no legs
to travel back, you see.

She was willing to trade her all, just to have
a glance...
if the lamb in her courtyard, did give birth to
an ewe,

nearby the gossamer stream? If the bakery
before which her
husband was gunned down sold *samoon* bread
still?

The white rosary beads, in silent rotation of
agony and hope,
split between her fingers, threaded her curled
wakeful anguish.

'*Even when you 're gone, the land still seeks you*',
she said. And the wind
called out her name. She did not know what to do

with what was left of her. I wonder now: did she
ever embark from
her boat? Did she ever leave her land? Did she
ever arrive to this

foreign shore?

Why then, did, her heart throb elsewhere?
My mother is now me.
I search for places where stories could be
found. Stories that came

before me, in a land where nothing was broken,
no one ripped apart.

Published in The Crossings, *October 2023*

CP SURENDRAN

Invitation
(For Sonu)

Put out with wine the heart's old, purple fire; wait.
Watch an absence thrive white in the wild jasmine
Breaking out on vines. Come in April when the house is
On fire. Or in dark June when the lone boy up in the loft
Flings crushed rain against the windowpane.
Or in November when leaves chilled yellow by the light
Of a dead star tremble and fall, scattering bug-eyed ants.
Come any time really, the moon here is mortgaged
To silence. Now that nothing can be said or done
Perhaps you will consider staying on for coffee, sun.

Published in Wholeness Review, *Canada, Aug 2023*

DEBMALYA
Spider

A spider has eight legs. Of course, you know this. You had learnt it in school when you were all of five. It was a day trebled by crashing rains. Mrs. White had shown an animated spider to prove her point. You held this tiny fact carefully in your hands and added it to your museum of animal facts. Eight wiggly legs, school no longer mortar and pestle, no longer scrubbed belly, liver-spinach, blind burrows under blankets. You wondered what pants would fit them. Eight boots to go hunt flies. A thought kicks off with all eight of its legs taking flight. You wanted a cobweb city to live in, to meet its spiders for lunch at a mosquito cafe. You practised webbing from your wrists in case Mrs. White was a Green Goblin. How you liked cobwebs back then! Soft invisible things running through the air, brushing against your face sometimes, summer melting on the saddle of time. How you wished you could invent softness out of thin air, and call it a home.

Published in Anthropocene Poetry, *December 2023*

DEEPA AGARWAL

Dysgraphia

Alphabets disperse
like leaves wrenched from a bough.
Rebellious children embracing chaos,
willfully dismembering meaning.
Unperturbed, mother tree watches,
knowing the sap of meaning
still courses in her veins,
impervious to the tsunami's onslaught.

Published in Setu, *September 2023*

DEVASHISH MAKHIJA
'fathers'

they wait on scooters
at right angles to the sun
measuring the slowness of
the summer heat
against the rapidly approaching bright
future they wish upon their sons.

they spend sparse holidays
folding old newspapers into
paper boats,
assuring their adventurous little boys
that love when shaped
this way does not capsize.

they steal money put aside
by mothers for
potatoes and rice – those comics
may not fill the stomach
but fathers seem to know that
it's the heart that needs
filling; stomachs can be trained to adjust.

and when their little boy
squats like a bird
turned to the window light
hungrily pecking at that comic, his little heart
skipping like a flat pebble across
the water of his
childhood, his father watches,
his heart full now,

hoping this could stay
exactly this way
forever; but knowing it
will not be so, he turns,
walks away, measuring
the slowness of his stride
against the rapidly approaching
shadows of
eventuality.

Published in The Punch Magazine, *March 2023*

DIPANJALI ROY
Earth, I'm Lying When I Tell You

The last time that I'm pinned down by a man, I'm twenty-three. Lying
on his new mattress on his new bed in his old room in his old house, we are
an almost. An accident. An *anything gets me hard these days*. Everything
with him is about factuality. The hard facts of the body now pinned to form.
Epiphany, tumbling hard against my sternum. Guilt, dripping down the slope
of his shoulders as rocks from a scree. I am so hopelessly in love with a moment.
I am so broken by its return. Paralysed by the parentheses, it is so easy to forget
the lesser woman of myself lying on his bed, lying in his car, lying about an entire
bottle of gin downed in my room after our fight in front of my friends at the bar.
Nothing to do with me, per se. I'm lying enough for the both of us. I'm refusing
to look him in the eye. In the brackets of blame, I imagine that his hand brushing
my ribcage is encyclopaedic. Unaffected. Pristine. He's only looking for directions.
He's devoted only to discovery. For eons unfolding, men have touched the earth
and found the right words to tell wonder apart from wound. Even here, just past
the window of his blue room, there is the hard cascade of laburnum pouring her
heart out to the ground in lavish racemes. Looking out the windows of other years,
now, I can't remember the slant of his voice as a boy in his kitchen asking me why
I like the smell of cloves in tea. All of it ends when it ends. *There*. With the kettle
still whistling so hard on the stove. *There*. With the long shadow of our time tilting
against the slow sundial of my girlhood as woman, as wound, as a planet pinned
to the orbit of her days. *Here*. With the axis extending, I'm trying to remember
the sun in your eyes. *Here*. I'm lying when I tell you I've forgotten the way.

Published in Wildness, *Issue 31, August 2023*

DURGA PRASAD PANDA
Eyes Walking on Manipur Streets

Breasts, too, have eyes
That hardly open, copper brown

And protruded round.
Like the eyes of a newborn

Baby, they can't tolerate
Too much of daylight.

If they had their ways
They would have seen the entire world

In a blink. Instead, like Gandhari,
They chose a self-imposed blindness.

May be it is better this way. Because
Whenever breasts open their fiery eyes

As they did, walking naked
In broad daylight on the streets

Of Manipur, the whole of mankind
Simply burns into ashes.

Published in Outlook, *12th Aug 2023*

FEBY JOSEPH
The Second Kiss

– The first was an accident;
a dare at playtime…
A forgotten break – forgotten
school & time. The second

happened in the middle
of a nightmare; I walked
the church alone
when suddenly

– Sunday; some time
after mass… I was talking
and my Sunday-School mate
surprised me; cut me

off mid-sentence –
with his lips – vanilla…
leftover from the ice cream
The church had

– distributed; in a forgotten nook
of a forgotten book filled
with my amnesia notes; I remembered
and still do… The slant

of sun; the hypotenuse
of the afternoon; the F-sharp
a myna sang; the air spicy
with carnation; my heart

– in fermata; the stillness
of our lips; the counterpoint
of blood and winds; only my ears
could hear, and then, he –

moved back; a hesitant smile
crumbling, till my smile
soothed *his* edges with
my eye-kisses; silent

– we knew, we knew; this dream
would remain a nightmare
in the nook of a church;
we walked back. We didn't

hold hands; *(we did that
later)* and walked back;
monsters into a hall
full of saints –

Published in The Bombay Literary Magazine, *Issue 54, April 2023*

GAURI AWASTHI
Collected Vision

Months after we've been allowed to go to the beach again,
you drive us to the closest one, past the shell-pink azaleas

just outside of town. Listening to a podcast on green parakeets
you remember the wild blackberries that grew on the farm

in Abbottabad, a mountain town all the way across Indian ocean.
You plucked from a dangling tree with a friend, *how wildly they grew,*

black and drooping, and how you could just pluck them as you liked.
It is in this moment we whisper-list to each other our vision for our world:

No tulip farm photo opportunities, just wild tulips ungrazed by buildings
and cement slabs. No rainforests burnt for the want of crops. Just foragers,

picking what grows slowly and softly. No apple orchard driveways to pick
fresh produce in plastic baskets. Just glowing apples unsprayed by pesticide.

May egrets fish from the gulf waters and dance to the sound of waves. May
the salmon and persimmons be full of color and a smell so orange that it peels

off our hands. May we always find a way to drive past ocean towns. May we
never find dead whales on this beach again. You driving slower than clouds,

whisper: may we always find conch shells to hear the sound of our world
as it echoes and echoes.

Published in Epiphany Magazine, *Fall/Winter 2023.*

GAYATRI LAKHIANI CHAWLA
Home with Wheels

Two cans of cat food were all that was left
maybe some leftover Paska from last night's dinner
and raw tender Salo perhaps.
How can one pack one's home in a haversack?
Pack the sunshine that bathed the kitchen
the laughter of a warm living-room
where the family ate together
serving both bread and salt to the guests
at the dining table.
One to enhance prosperity
the other to wade off bad luck
both in a state of delirium now.
The night before the war
two rose candles brightened the dark room
who would have guessed that would be the last meal
sometimes unpredictability is a noose of death
for a world suffering from aphasia and blindness.

Notes
Paska- a bread native to Ukraine
Salo – Traditional Ukrainian food

Published in Rhetorica 25, *September 2023*

GEETHA RAVICHANDRAN

Measuring

Those were days, when the kitchen did not have a clock or a timer. But we soon learnt that time is the ultimate essence. Batter needs time to rise. Curd appears only when it is set and left unshaken for the equivalent of a night's sleep. Milk has to be stirred slowly to allow it to caramelize. Frying takes a quick flick of the wrist, else there would be charred remains for a meal. Like in the ripening of fruits, flavours in the simmering casserole yield to time's craft. It has a value beyond measure.

brewing tea
the misty aromas
of patience

Published in Failed Haiku Issue 86, *Feb 2023*

GOPAL LAHIRI
Living Inside

1.

I read water in water,
the house is swelling like a sack,

Outside, the tall tree unbolts its mossy smile,
pink flowers show their scarlet tongues
confirming the bed boundaries.

2.

The light will uncover cracks now
as someone writes dark narratives.

A door knitting the rainstorm,
a window scripts shrinking space
for every vanished land.

3.

The brightness spreads like a stain,
a pinpoint affix me to the wall.

The floor holds your face in its marble veins,
something in us breathes
only when we move away.

Published in The Undiscovered Journal, *Singapore, Issue #1,*
October 2023

GOPIKRISHNAN KOTTOOR
Our Ambassador Car

Our brand new Ambassador car
Was all painted ivory.
I remember how then,
I danced round and round
Like it was a golden tambourine.

Mother kept jasmine flowers
Hanging upon its laughing bonnet
Young smoking father,
He broke two coconuts upon its engine
To drive away the devils and the gremlins.
And our driver stomped into the hard steering
Driving his Bela kiss mush,
Lit jog sticks, and pinned them there into the air vent
Like she was a girl who had to be perfumed before first night.

We turned the yellow thing
Into a pinned lemon butterfly.

Well, now with hands gone shaking,
This morning I wake from sleep
In a dream of dead dogs & red kitten heads
Rolling from the old school bookshelf,
With the ghosts of my father and mother
Framed upon dead skin on the wall
and love
Steaming from its boiling radiator;

My childhood dead in its red oxide dickey.

Published in Wingword International Poetry Prize, *longlist, 2023.*

HUZAIFA PANDIT
we remember when there was only the rain

We remember when there was only the rain, nothing
but the rain. The rain chain stitched itself to our hearts
till our hearts hung out their crimson shadows
to dry in the famished sun. We too remember when there was only
the silence, nothing but silence. We lent silence a language
but nobody came to console us. Only the birds born out of our rubble
wept in our ruins and time hurried past us
with our yesterdays in its luggage.
We forgot when we tumbled out of tomorrow with
the gauze of bleeding clouds flung over our
slumped shoulders. Our destinies were shattered on
the pavements, and the soldiers picked up pieces of
to use as looking mirrors and stroke their guns
with the pride of careless death.

We remember when there were only the shadows, nothing
but the shadows. We cremated our names on water
to reach the other side where you stood waiting with open
arms in the land of your siege and my siege,
the perfume of ripe wheat in your moist eyes. Be
our shadow between the two wars on our glass maps. Take
us to your gardens laden with cherry blossom, sprinkle us
with rose-water and comb our wheat in the prisons of
your names. What was the point of your waiting, who do we
await in the long winter? Did the poets not warn us to lock
our sleep weary doors, as all promises stood broken. Nobody came,
the shikara wala laments, and I complete the verse:
Nobody will now come here, nobody.

Our poem is in your manacled hands and can comb
its fingers through our forgotten songs sung
when we return dead from destiny's road. We
kiss the poem, surrender our hearts and ask:
Who are you? Who are we?

Published in Parcham, *Third Issue, April 2023*

IMTIAZ DHARKER
The Show

Colonel Blair and his Family and an Indian Ayah
by Johann Zoffany 1786

Not an *ayah*, you want to say, a *child*.

The portrait painter gives them
a noble version of themselves to take back home
and hang above a marble fireplace.

Husband and wife clasp hands, dead centre,
flanked by porcelain daughters. They have allowed
the extra girl into the frame. They do not mind

if her clothes are frayed and mended,
washed and washed again, pounded to softness
on a stone. They think of themselves as kind

masters. She has been given a cat to hold.
On the wall is a landscape with elephant
and scenes of savage customs:

a widow on her way to a funeral pyre,
a tableau of torture. This
will be a conversation piece in Perthshire.

The child is wide-eyed, caught in a performance
that goes on for years in polite rooms
full of rustling silk.

It makes a sound like scavengers
circling in the undergrowth.

Published in the RA Royal Academy Special Issue Entangled Pasts,
Winter 2023

INAM HUSSAIN BEGG MULLICK

Inamorato Takes a Walk

A dark bird
gainsays the storm's
hammer,
our zinced love
is warm;
the fish magnify summer.

Your body to mine,
the magpie flies.

*

The sky is rubbed by fire,
we observe
the blood dancer's gyr
and saunter along dream roads of rock rose and ursine cloud song.

I pluck a dream
from the midnight tree.

*

The wind's opera is a lunar saponification,
the crooner's horse has a moonlight saddle.
Sprites
sing in white,
sashay across
scarified skin, I remember jinns bowing to Allah on celestial hills.

Published in Lothlorien Poetry Journal, *23rd June 2023*

INDU PARVATHI

The Countries of Sleep

The restless sink in their beds, they fitfully sleep. (Walt Whitman, The Sleepers)

                              Are
                        sleep nets
                          sparse
          dense   or selfish
         in their   weaves?
      After shedding   grime, night-fears
  hide in sleep's design to change   its yarn-count to take me to another
sand every time I am caught, choices   flutter on poles, microbial moans from far
    out in the sea, break to mend   break to mend, I am acupunctured
  with fractured ditties to invoke   vision, the hero turns villain, a dying
   candle flame, the bedspread,   a Rorschach blot, safest
         to locate at the   rib   of noiselessness
        as intent splinters   into words, meaning
          yet to emerge,   the future, past's
        imprint, I shape   the dark into a flag
        tasselled with   all the stars
                          from
                      the nights
                      to come.

Published in THE SEVENTH WAVE, *22nd June 2023*

IRWIN ALLEN SEALY
Paradiso

Angels in lycra glide by on the riverbank
the phalanx on the bicycle path repeated in black water

upside down. Drifting ducks vex that mindless orange synchrony
of pumping knees with bald impassive heads of iridescent green.

Ne-ver-the-less!—the ducks quack—should blood
well up on mown grass from a heroic last stand hereabouts

it is given to you to breathe in only the given moment.
A balsam poplar shakes out resplendent hair

leans into a magnolia in fragrant bloom
each great waxen chalice not proof of heaven

but heaven itself. The mallard chief becomes his feather cloak.
Three of his cohort ride the current, one paddles upstream

getting nowhere, two graze on a trove of duckweed bottoms up.
Midway through the latter end of life I find myself

drowsing in clover under an ancient willow
by a placid stream at the edge of the known world

beset by dandelions on the brink of paradise.

Published in Poetry at Sangam, *January, 2023*

JIM WUNGRAMYAO KASOM
Philosophy of a Mountain Man

I'm a hunter.
I'm a listener.

When I hear a mountain deer bark
I stop sharpening my spear
and keep it for another day.

I can smell bad omen like rotten eggs.

I've learned to live with the land,
not from the land, and sometimes
the mountain sings back to me.

Published in Cradling Memories of My Land, *Red River,*
November 2023.

JOHANNES MANJREKAR
Le Dernier Metro

The millipede is black with regularly spaced yellow markings. Its resemblance to a train at night is enhanced by the smooth way it glides along the ground on its many wonderfully coordinated legs. Suddenly I am transported back to a night many years ago.

A couple of minutes out of Neral station very little was visible other than the fading station lights. Though my father was sure of the general direction, the narrow paths across the slushy ground were difficult to pick out in the feeble light of our torch. 'It's just ten minutes from the station,' my father kept insisting, but we blundered through the darkness for what seemed like hours before my father exclaimed, 'Ah!' All our torch showed us was a bunch of trees, but they were mango trees. Two minutes later, we were knocking on the door of the owner's mud-and-wood house. The kerosene lantern-lit face that appeared at the door abruptly went from suspicion to delight, and half an hour later we were polishing off the last of the bhakri and smoke-tinged vaal.

Later at night, my father and I sat out on a charpoy under the mango trees. 'That must be the last Karjat local,' my father remarked as we watched the near-empty train glide through the darkness. 'Le Dernier Metro' I think now, decades later.

The hug he gave me before I fell asleep that night was perhaps the closest this matter-of-fact rationalist man who was my father ever came to expressing what he never put into words.

flashing fireflies
the silence broken only
by crickets

Published in Jacarandas are a Deep Shade of Blue, *Red River,*
February 2023

JONAKI RAY

Who Does this Air Belong to?

The border between Delhi and Noida,
and Gurugram and Faridabad, for once, has
smoothened, with blinking vehicles' lights, leading
the entire Delhi-NCR turned-into-a-Nigambodh like *ghat*.

    This is a world where the highway signs, the towers,
    the *sabzimandis*, the metro coaches and its tracks,
    —are reduced to playground toys, uniformly glazed
    with an ochre shade that integrates the Yamuna into the sky.

Who does this air belong to?
a cry scrambles to the sky, silencing the birds,
as the world seems to be ending, the city's children
are choking, despairing, their lungs charcoaling.

    Thousands of years ago, a Roman emperor
    had once declared: "Three things belong to everyone
    —air, running water, and the sea." Back then, the world
    was deemed to end where the horizon straightened.

Today, the world seems to be ending as the
air keeps getting indexed, the numbers keep measuring visibility,
the news keeps anthemizing particulates and NO2, comparing
warring skies and the children dying there to this city and its sky.

    As if that makes the world seeming to end anywhere palatable.
    On the Delhi roads, the houses, offices, animals, trees,
    traffic, people—are all disappearing into a haze,
    one-by-one. Everything has flamed and reduced

to rubble and ruins, and now, only ash remains,
clogging our throats, our lungs, our bones, and their marrow,
squeezing life out, slowly, while children keep getting strangled.
Yet, no one answers, *who does this air belong to*

Published in Hindustan Times, *November 6, 2023*

JYOTIRMOY SIL
Nakshi Kantha

Eroded moments,
A forgone raga…
Grandmother weaving nakshi kantha;
The fluent flow of thread
With its furry stitched turns
Embroidered mystique images—
As if some archaic folktales
Entwined with oblivious faces;
Unknown humming of some inner voids,
Some tale of tales.
My eyes charmed
Admiring the colourful curves,
Narrowed furry red shades;
Its mapped edges
Harboured her melancholy
Hymns of her deep ignominy.

(Nakshi Kantha is a Bengali traditional hand-weaved embroidered quilt.)

Published in Setu Bilingual Magazine, *June 2023 Issue*

K. SRILATA
What if, for a day, that square sky outside your window was yours?

What if, for a day, that square sky outside your window
was yours?
The birds it hugs, their flight,
the lakes they visit in continents you will now never go to –
what if, the joys that unfurl outside your window,
were yours?
What if, for a day, the hearts of bird watchers,
those lovers of winged creatures that stand still and won't stay,
what if, for a day, their hearts, wide open skies
beating in all the continents you will now never go to,
were yours?

Published in From my Window: The Window Journal, *June 2023*

KABIR DEB
Smell

I lure the porcupines - the bigger than life
ones - it has always been my desire
to pierce the sky; laugh at how
it can be stopped, robbed
from being the mighty
roof -- the hand on my
forehead is bigger than it;
- her hands wrapping me like a
promise - a thing bigger than a star,
older than silence -- love needs a victory
over everything that makes me run
like blood; she can make a cut
where I need a shortcut to
her tongue - the taste
of my yesterday has a
bitter meeting, confidently
spoken slurs, the piece of her
delicately made lingerie - I may run
out of breath; I won't run out of memory.

Published in Wives Anthology, *28/10/2023*

KANDALA SINGH
Narangi

I roll my eyes when you say *orange*
in your American accent.
It is not an orange, but a tiny globe

that peoples every winter
in my city. You reduce my narangi

childhood to thick English marmalade,
your tongue folding over winters

I spent picking minute
spheres from a garden in Delhi.

We would pile them up,
my mother & I, peel each one
painstakingly, tears running

as the sharp tang
hit our nostrils. The masala
on the pan, sizzling,

and that colour
just before we popped
them in the pickle jar

—not saffron, not sunset,
but somewhere between

the valleys of Kashmir
and a Delhi winter afternoon.

I can taste it tonight, sharp
citrus retort on my tongue
as you tell me *no big deal,*

just revise the Hindi
words out of your poems.

Listen. There are some things
you cannot taste.

Published in Frontier Poetry, *3rd Nov 2023*

KASHIANA SINGH

Instructing a Yoga Class

Step outside this coquettish altar
a container
lounge into yourself   deepening into spine
ease your breath   let it unwind in interludes
nudge every thought towards its navel center

You are gripping the sides of calloused hide
fingers claw into the backs of arthritic knees
perhaps, an attempt to run the warmth of palms
up and down your leg's   torso in a balasana

Examine awkwardness of breath   it is a river
imagine you are afloat   in unnamedgalaxies
allow every person in shavasana on their mat
to free rise   let them also be a constellation

Find afterlife in craters   touch their hollow
make space for the woman adjacent too
browse barefoot into the frangipani forest
follow in footprints of a mycorrhizal web

Walk along forgotten pathways   its last light
inside glowworms, beauty rearranged slowly
humming seamstress of skies as you gather
cracked skulls from smoldering pyre lights

Published in stonepoetryjournal, *May 2023*

KAVITA EZEKIEL MENDONCA
The Dancing Professor

Seated in the middle row
of the old, University classroom
on hard benches that hurt the body
one window to let in the hot humid Bombay air
Surrounded by eager friends
Hungry for the truths of Literature and life
I watched the bespectacled professor
in his maroon khadi kurta climb on to the dais
(He had blue, ochre, brown khadi kurtas too
In his collection)
A different color for each day of the week
Each lecture colored by a different hue.

He was teaching rhythm and meter in poetry
Iambic, trochaic, spondaic, anapestic, dactylic.

From the dais to the front of the class
He began to gallop like a horse
He explained it was called Anapestic rhythm
Also known as the galloping rhythm.

The students applauded
I hung my head and averted his gaze
I was young and I felt embarrassed,
There was only one exit
I was seated far from that escape.

You see, the professor in the colorful kurta
Was my father!

I had gone shopping with him
to the local Cottage Industries store
to buy the style of kurtas he loved
Perhaps I should take some of the blame for the loud colors
Though I did try to have him buy the cream-colored ones.

At home I asked why he galloped in front of the students
He simply said 'Poetry is a dance of words.'

Published in Verse-Virtual, *January 2023*

KINJAL SETHIA
Problem

The house help calls her periods a problem.
Mera problemhai na, didi
aajmein late aayegi.
I wonder at her words.
The urge to correct her, emancipate her.
Empower her. Tell her to wear the menstrual
cycle proudly. Not to hide her feminism.
Embrace it.

A tin shed that holds Mercurial temperatures,
a roof that leaks on her bed every monsoon.
A communal tap that works only at night,
a queue pregnant with fights. Rags
that stain and stink despite her strength.

I empty my cup, sanitise it.
And shut up because she has a problem.

Published in Issue 9 of Usawa Literary Review, *June 2023*

KINSHUK GUPTA

DNA Extraction

Morning, 8—you drape the white coat,
dust settling on its cuffs like Olympic rings,
threads flailing from buttonholes.

You wear purple gloves, touch the DNA model
that reminds you of your mother's braided hair.
Sit on the cold and cranky stool, crane your neck

in the cabinet, blue light falling like a halo
above your head. There are blood vials,
named and numbered, and your hands move

with robotic precision to rupture the RBCs,
to vibrate them on the vortex, to rotate the turbid
mixture at 10,000 rpm. This is how everybody starts

you are told, that research is watching a forest bloom
from the seeds that dripped from the corner
of your mouth as you bit into the heart of a tomato—

no different than making love. That you wake up
to the clockface making an obtuse angle, your legs tangled
with his like a cat's cradle pattern, and wish to peep

into his heart of fern. That while walking through the markets
where women in tucked-up sarees, haggle in brassy voices
over prices of rohu and rawas, you hold his hand tightly

without any reason. That the Buddha's sermon—the one
when he says that if you love a flower, you won't pluck it—
makes you think he never found love.

Loving is dreaming of a home on the land
rattled by everyday earthquakes
like this process of extracting DNA

where you pipette, incubate, rotate and wait
for that squirrel of hope—that when you will dim
the light and put the slab under the UV monitor,
a thick purple band will illuminate.

Published in RHINO Poetry, *2023*

KIRITI SENGUPTA
Haiku

i
descent of grace
the priest unburdens
the donation box

ii
the postbox
recedes to rust —
a lost art

iii
plagiarism
the author examines
the reader's memory

Published in Indian Literature *(#337 | September-October 2023),* Sahitya Akademi

LINA KRISHNAN
Lemon Vipassana

The yellow globe awaits its destruction
And my resurgence

Poles sliced, pips knocked off
The equator held firmly between thumb and finger

Now, the river follows its course
No part left unscathed by its astringent medley
Cell after cell after cell wakes to life

Published in the RIC Journal in *May 2023*

MADHU RAGHAVENDRA
Vague

We stand beside each other
watching a child dance.
The silence between the words
in your language
and the silence between the words
in my language
effortlessly sound the same.
It is the sounds of words
that must work hard
very, very hard, to make it clear
whom to hate
when you choose hat
You must be attentive
very, very attentive
because hate is vague
very, very vague
so much so that
if we are not careful
it could end up being directed
at the dancing child
that is yet to learn a language.

Published in There Are No Others, *Red River, 9th March, 2023*

MALASHRI LAL
Hawa Mahal

Who sits behind those tiered windows
Arched like Ram's bow
Waiting to tremble into action
For a hunt yet to start?
A princess in royal blue
The colour of Diwali
Peers from the shadows
Looking eagerly at the carriages below
Thirsting for a paramour
Not yet known.

> Cloistered girlhood,
> Guarded puberty,
> Controlled womanhood
> How did she learn to dream
> Of love and desire?
> Was it from the legends of Krishna
> Intricately drawn on the walls?
> Was it her prayers which held hidden meaning
> In pursuing the call of the flute?

Published in Mandalas of Time: Poems. *Hawakal Publishers, 2023.*

MAMANG DAI
In Memoriam

In the past many things happened.
It rained, and we plunged into the river,
our hearts in our mouths,
ready to turn into a current.

Time was a river
wearing a headdress of ice.
A flashing summer
with the face of the long cloud
camouflaged with light,
bending low,
when a small town suddenly fell asleep
as the sun dipped down
one afternoon.

Stronger than illness or injury
I thought we would grow old together.
How can it be that we will not visit
those winding places wet with rain,
when there is more to find out
about freedom and love.

In secret we dreamt of new beginnings,
of work we would do.
Who knows—
Time is a narrative of finding words,
losing them,
to find them again in another place,
waiting with the wind and stars
in the mountains where we were born,

for the short walk together
to retrieve those stones with names:
Adi Pasi, Siang, Wakro, Liromoba.

Published in White Shirts of Summer, *Speaking Tiger Books, 2023*

MANDAKINI BHATTACHERYA
Tree-True

The staccato rhythm
washed upon dazed sleep - chop chop chop.
The tree wanted to shout - Stop!
It was hushed by more blows.
Down dropped the mangoes
on the prickly brown leaves
faking a red-carpet.

The roving axe came near my windows.
The morning bled white and green
with shiny water apples,
feasted upon now only by crows.
The *mynahs, bulbuls, koyels* stayed away.
Only the small woodpecker worked lustily,
stunned at the gaping, bare boughs.

Loss is a green canopy
that shaded me from prying eyes.
Loss is a tree,
a fairy-whisperer, soothing me to sleep,
cut down to size.

Published in EKL Review *Issue 10, August 2023*

MANI RAO
Without Touching

Unless by heart is meant the anatomical,
believers do not use the word
in poems. Believers of

Precision, we
who measure words, distances
between words and things
they try to touch.

Calibrating thus I walked to the river-bank
where countless hearts of stone
protested the analogy.

I picked up one and a cold wave
tore along my arm to crash, not left
of centre, but in the exact center
of my chest. Then froze into a knot.

Hearts sink because blood is thicker than water.
Don't I keep on searching for that heart of gold.
The day I stepped upon a broken heart barefoot.

Upon a rock, a heron, and another heron,
upside down, immersed in the water
without touching.

Then without warning soared
my winged heart.

Published in Verseville, *issue XXXVI, December 2023*

MEENA CHOPRA
The Silent Glory of Port Credit by Night

Bright beam drizzles down
from the lighthouse
Shimmering waters on rocks
Breaking the silence of silver-patinas.
Ashen moonlight.

Stars sentinels.
Soft gentle breeze on my cheeks.

Like the water
I am swamped in silence.
The heavens fall
And the sky is empty.

Published in Soul Spaces Poems on Cities, Towns & Villages, *by* Authorspress, 2023

MEENAKSHI MOHAN
Van Gogh's Silent Cry

Today, in the museums
when you walk
in Van Gogh's immersive experience
and become a part of my paintings --
The Starry Night, Sunflowers, the Irises, and many others
you marvel at my creations.
I move around the world,
you spend millions,
in owning my work.

Where were you,
when I struggled with life?
I was a starving artist
with no money to buy food
I would sip on turpentine.
A poor artist toiling
with mental and physical health.
You did not see me cry
when I cut my ears.

Where were you in my lonely hours
when my every breath craved for help?
Today, you look at my Self Portrait
and say, "Here is the famous artist --
Vincent Van Gogh!"

When alive
I was struggling on the earth.

If only you had heard my
Silent Cry, then!

Published in Confluence *UK, November/December 2023*

MENKA SHIVDASANI
Confluence

At the point where the Gomti and Saryu meet,
every stone is a tribute, every ripple a new breath.
The roaring rivers have journeyed
down the mountain,
carving rigid landscapes,
navigating the waterfalls,
seeking their spaces in crevices of rock.
Now they curve, gentle into each other's sides
sharing stories that no one else can know,
mingling memories of silver oak and pine.
Who can tell where one begins,
who can tell where
it flows into the other?

As the decades have streamed by,
we have changed our course
and yet remained together,
smoothening the rough edges
of boulders on this riverbed,
meandering along the shoreline,
shifting the soil.
Tributaries have flowed in,
distributaries disappeared
but we have gone on,
inseparable between the banks.

Someday, in a far-off land,
when rain dries mid-air
as the sun burns too bright,
we will leave our memories
in pebbles on the sand

and though selfie-taking crowds
may step on them,
it will not matter, for we will
have left our mark,
bringing forests to life
feeling our breath in the breeze.

We have moved mountains,
though this secret is ours
and no one else will know.

Published in *CAESURAE MANA, July 2023*

MRINALINI HARCHANDRAI

Her Voice as a Thangka Painting

The cloud unscrolling across the textile of lapis lazuli nerves is how silence explodes. Unframed, raw-edged, a wheel with the long strokes of lifetimes.

The lama says dark knows itself by the shaft of light. Her light is the radical counterforce to the mandala of caverns she was twisted out of.

When darkness of apprehension falls across the monastery, a thousand eyes grow on the silken relief of her body.

Mystique is a closed-off posture that falls between the Bodhisattva and her desire, between the hop of a beetle or birdflight. Defence is a stylistic trajectory of cause and effect.

She weaves in the secret symbols for love, wisdom, peace, anger, abundance, invites the Lord of Death to emboss the golden foil of time. Geometry is her insight into the brocaded wheel of becoming, an invitation to step beneath the veil and open another sense quite smoothly removed from algorithms of the gridded course.

Published in The Dalhousie Review *Vol 102 No 2, 05-06-2023*

MUGDHA SINHA
Hair-Do Status

straight hair, deliberately
and profusely oiled, in a
single plait neatly arrayed

coiffured hair, loosely
left open with a single red
rose ceremoniously perched

hair cut short, reduced to
a bob, with no embellishments
dangling commitments or strings attached

notice how hairdos reveal
a women's mind, in sync with
her meandering marital journey

Published in Postcard Poems, *Red River, New Delhi, February 2023*

MUSTANSIR DALVI

Tamazight – an Amazi'ɣs poem

Sand is no longer captured
by the litham covering our faces.
The cloth remains unsullied
as if never used.
We wander the Maghreb,
speak, and are misunderstood
in tongues other than our own.
Our mouths, forever dry.
What would it be like
if I spoke only to myself?
What could I say?
What sense would I make?
My mind empties
like one half of an hourglass,
dripping obstinately into the other
that is the Sahara.
My throat is serrated with desire.
I want to tell you of the Fezzan,
of its wadis, of its waters sweet as dates,
of the tattoos that make our women.
You meet me halfway, in your voice:
every greeting, every civility
mediated by the monoglossia
of your shrunken world.

Published in The Silk Road Anthology: Nano Poems for Africa,
The Silk Road Literature, Cairo 2023

N SEHAR
In Urdu, a ghazal

Saunth, Sauf, Sarso bought near a *Baagh* in Urdu,
English being too heavy on the tongue, mother cooks *saag* in Urdu.

Aleef for *ashq, asbaab; meem* for *Mazloom.*
In language, mother mothers horror, her voice cracks in Urdu.

Austen, Bronte, Woolf are too far-fetched a dream,
Parveen Shakir is what she stacks in Urdu.

Mother presses father's clothes but piles hers up on shelves.
Often mother wraps grief in plastic bags in Urdu.

Mother has a *shauhar* in all flesh and bones,
A lover is what she lacks in Urdu.

Mother's devotion drifts through air at the crack of every dawn.
She bleeds the ghosts and knits them in cotton racks in Urdu.

Mother curses scalp, calls her ageing skin a diseased map.
She will dig herself a grave; won't cut herself a slack in Urdu.

Cheap labour, choice poverty, barred in her own body.
The canvas of inheritance is all-black in Urdu.

Mother believes to have too many births in the past,

In not even one she could reclaim her tongue back in Urdu.

Published in Gulmohar Quarterly, *Issue 12, December 2023*

NAMRATA PATHAK
For Passah Who Reads Water

Your palms break the pact of peace with the river,
stir the surface with an angry growl, and I,
a useless bystander, sound exactly like you:

"A liquid has a definite volume and it cannot be compressed.
Liquids do not have a definite shape but acquire the shape
of the vessel in which it is placed."

And
of all the states of matter, liquid is more subject
to violence and deceit, Passah. Tell me,
would you?

How do you read water?
How do you write its faithlessness on the skin?
Turn its opacity into words?

Does water sit cross-legged on your page too,
not moving an inch right, not moving an inch left?

Does it tease the margin out of every page,
bringing river to land, land to river?

How do you translate this reticence into light, sky, stars?

When this blueness splinters into thousand types
of hopelessness
in the palm of a lonely poet
how do you turn water into poetry, Passah?

Published in Muse India, *Issue No. 109, May-June, 2023*

NAMRATHA VARADHARAJAN

The Pile

On
day one,
you don't fold
that on handkerchief
because you are tired of doing
it all the time. And everyone you
know, lets it slide. It's a chore, it's
not gonna make a world of difference
if it is in or out: just a wolf-whistling in
your direction, or a brush past against you
on the bus— a single sock can just be thrown
away, maybe, even a few clothes could be folded
later, tomorrow is another day. Dumping them at
the back of the closet is always an option. It won't be
right in your face that way. The squeeze of one boob,
a pinch, or one slap on the butt in a dark alley, could be
buried under there— behind the stack of laundered relationships,
well-ironed memories, and closed antique almirahs. you let it pile… A
casual uninvited hand on the waist here, a dress draping the chair
there, you let it pile…and when the coat stand can no longer bear its
own weight, you out the uncle who Your family swept under the sofa in the
living room and it backfires honour in your direction. So, you let it pile.

Now,

you sit alone, in a closed room, binging on ice-cream, wearing sweat
pants with chilly stains on them, cause they are relatively clean. you let it pile, and it
piles and piles till there are mountains of mouths stuffed with all the world's single
socks (used and unwashed), even a teacher dumps his laundry on your bed, under the
covers, in your head, And, now the stuffing in your mouth, down your throat, is the
longest, most colourful string of magician scarves that everyone claps for, shoved in
with a crowbar, by big hands, bigger, till it is in your oesophagus, (and do they swim in
your intestines yet?) and when you try to scream (the same old story), in this ocean
of hashtags, you are just one news article, that they'll scroll over.

Published in Usawa Literary Review, *Issue 9, May 22, 2023*

NEHA R. KRISHNA
Collecting Prayers

prayers are broken wings
of many butterflies
collected in between the pages of old books.
slowly losing their colours to
the pages
that have cocooned them.
clouding the alphabets,
spaces, and
every character
that were supposed to breathe.
smudging the meaning of words
with their remains, and
staining the beige pages
with deaths.

Published in Quail Bell Magazine, *September 2023*

NIKITA PARIK

To Woman is to Witness

changes in set semantics,
the word guilt, for instance.

Guilt. /gɪlt/. Noun.
Definition:

a grenade
bombing this side of 20s
for not having understood
our mothers sooner-

not having,
for instance, held their overwhelmed
gazes,

scanned that the fatigue
lining their eyes
was frustration,

was helpless anger,
was a silent plea,
was the chipping
of the body and soul
into exhausted bits,

was a question mark
on other nouns such as
dreams. purpose. worth.

To woman is to watch

emotive history
repeat itself:

These days,
after the sun slips off the horizon,
this house explodes.
Things not picked up after

their owners
feel like arson; garbage thrown into the bin
without the lining in place,
incendiarism.

Published in The Lake Poetry, *UK, 1st August 2023.*

NISHI CHAWLA
Dis-colored

Yesterday afternoon, the sun spoke to me,
Slowly, lazily, cheekily, carefully checking me
For aftereffects, with its flashbulb style scans;
I looked back at the glowing red, befuddled.

My captive soul knew a riptide for its message,
Why would I wear safety eyewear, for we are all
Birds in flight, loosened upon a fissured planet,
Branded by the color of our skin tone and type.

I cling to my roots that turns into a no answer,
Cut loose, my fate blooming in brown earth
My pain turns into a no response, like a black
Slash of lightening, somber messenger of fate.

I am my own little garden, content to be raking
My kind of grass, and the plants do not question,
Adrift in my shadow, nor 'of color 'or'which color,'
Those dreadful clocks of colorless seasons, sealed.

I hate the peace of coloring, and its weird lies,
Endured beyond the 'black like me 'poppings,
I scream with pain, squeak, throw buckets of water,
A voyager on green mountains, sun-blocked.

Published in The Bombay Review, *March 2023*

OINDRI SENGUPTA
December 7th

Some colours of white have dropped the sunset
at your window—
tinted with lights often seen around fishing boats
resigned at the shore.
As usual
you returned home with an evening
lost inside your bag a millennium ago.
Since then the door of your night
has been left ajar,
for the one who has lived with the heart of a twilight.
For yours has the dimension of a rose.
So you make elaborate arrangements
for the days to come,
while I carefully cross the months on the calendar.
And now.
as the soft winter sky lights up your room,
you sit at your desk
identifying words from an old painting,
and I watch you closely over your shoulder.
So that together we can measure,
at what pace a darkness would travel.

Published in *Dreich Magazine, Scotland*, September 2023

PERVIN SAKET

Word Problems for Ten Marks Each

(after Bhaskara II's 'Lilavati')

1. If, on a full moon night,
a boy, nineteen, climbs all forty-four steps
to flat B-205 and leaves
without getting my brother's number,
how many suns will it take
to feed courage to his feet again?

2. If Tap A can fill three buckets in a minute
and Tap B can fill half a bucket,
if Tap A is molded from ancient brass
and Tap B from mongrel alloy,
if Tap A belongs to the fourth bathroom of a bungalow
and Tap B to a cracked gas station basin,
what will the astrologer need to be paid
to see alignment in their stars?

3. If Firuza, of the straight A's
and curved waist, who has learned
to clasp her chemistry books to her chest,
is the regular source of optical data
to five pairs of unblinking, pursuant eyes,
how many weeks before her father
decides she doesn't
need college anymore?

4. If one two-armed man
can build half a wall in eight days
and one two-armed woman
can build three quarters of a wall in a dozen days,

how many walls will need to fall
before they hold the same number
of two-faced coins in their two hands?

5. (*Bonus Question*)
If Hari, who washes your car,
has to divide seven rotis and two onions
between five children,
explain why
Hari, who washes your car,
has to divide seven rotis and two onions
between five children.

Published in Aesthetica Magazine *(UK), December 2023.*

PRABHU S GUPTARA
Guru Paksha

As the moon through the branches
dances and shines
and weaves and ducks
as a lion hides

slinks
uses camouflage
springs
as a cat

plays
sidlesup
gives a little nip, claws
rubs himself against me, amiably

companionably
he rolls a dice
dangles a throne
turns on the music.

Who's the frog in the water, then
gradually being warmed, so
it doesn't jump out?
"Six million children in our country", I plead
"Aren't taught even to write or to read".
So let's teach them yoga!
"Eleven million children", I push
"Are dead every year for reasons that are entirely avoidable".

Let's plant trees!
I don't normally say boo, but today I am a loon.
"Twenty-five million children don't get the basics: milk or rice or bread!
Its living hell".

Let's organise a satsang
"Thirty-one million", I sin
"Do you understand, Guruji, what that means?!
"Can't find jobs".

Ah, do stop obsessing about such things
Concerning this world, which is merely maya.
He has me binned.
Instead, do your pranayama, then shout 'Jai Hind!'

His ways are a riddle as well as a rune,
Weaving and ducking, and ducking and weaving,
Dancing and shining, as through the trees, the moon.

Published in The Beacon, *June 2023.*

PRAMILA VENKATESWARAN
Exile is Not a Foreign Word

To understand exile, you don't have to look
further than the family down the street
who lost their home and all they owned,
including their pets, in a fire, or a foreclosure,
or the mass of people reaching their arms out
to rescuers who pull them out of the water
in the sudden hurricane that sweeps the coast
where you live, or the birds that drop dead
at your feet and you smell the smoke
of wild fire blazing through a forest up North.
You don't have to look far to understand exile
and homelessness. True, you still have a state
you claim as yours. But the sensation of being
in a vacuum, a dead zone, arises when your name
etched on an identity card or online records
cannot verify your existence, yes, that too
is the reality of anyone who swears by a country,
not to mention if your palms are charred
and your face alters with hurt.

Published in Long Island Quarterly, *2023.*

PRIYA SARUKKAI CHABRIA
Ambapali after meeting Gautama in Vaishali

Once a boat rowing
in a known direction
now unsure
of reaching shore

Rope of water
Lasso of breeze
            connects the banks

Craft a raft of light
of your body
            Pull to the other side

*

Every spot is the center
Which way to turn

Learn to walk again

*

Ancestors
of wood water air
have stood
on this alluvial soil

*

Pouring gloam
molts river's transparency
into amber mirror
Depth disappears

What else does light hide

*

Surrounded by forest's breath
like rudharsha seeds
strung on prayer
every step
taken away
is towards

*

Once lost in my own name

     mango sprout

which grew
into   tree   grove   forest
rustling skirts of gold

Published in Reliquiae (UK) *VOL 10, NO. 2, 2023*

PRIYANKA SACHETI
Tree Mother

A prickly platinum river
cracks the bruised sky in
two.
A tree mother dressed in bridal finery,
arms laden with moon flowers,
stands quietly, drenched in star rain.
By dawn, the ground beneath her feet
will be a city of broken dove wings.
The day the ground turns red,
the tree knows it is going to die:
one limb giving way after another
until all that will remain are
a handful of seeds
nesting inside married roots.
Every day,
knowing its abbreviated life
draws closer to its end,
the tree consoles itself with this:
If I could not walk in my lifetime,
I will bear children who will fly.

Published in The Selkie *(Scotland) on July 31st, 2023*

R SURESH BABU
Mosaic

My daughter has my eyes and I have inherited mine from my mom.
My eyes are always wet. Mom had smiling eyes. Dad used to call her an
apple of his eye. My husband called mine sparkling that hooked up
young men. He punched on my face when I applied mascara to my
eyes. I am waiting for Naina to sleep. Her eyes have curly lashes. The
surma on them will ward off evil eyes. dawn - dappled light
on the fawn 's body

Published in Usawa Literary Review, *Issue 9, June 2023*

RADHA CHAKRAVARTY
The Casket of Secret Stories

Paaner bata—bell metal casket
that once held grandmother's gossip, spicy
rumours of desire, heartbreak, longing, loss,
rolled in lime-smeared *paan*, betel leaf
flavoured with *supuri, lavanga, elaach,*
and sometimes a dash of *dokta,*
forbidden tobacco—loaded with sin,
mouth-watering ritual, daily rite
of chewing with relish upon
secret morsels of women's inner lives

In the delicious telling,
bright red juice trickling
from the mouth, staining
tongue and teeth, savouring
the covert knowledge
of what life felt like in dark corners
of the home's secluded inner quarters,
what the world on the outside looked like
from behind veils, screens,
barred windows and closed courtyards
where women's days began and ended,
leaving for posterity
this precious closed *kaansha* casket,
redolent with the aroma of lost stories

Published in Subliminal: Poems, *New Delhi, Hawakal, 2023*

RAHANA K ISMAIL
Crochet

Monsoon girled around to house her body, her long fingers drizzling
to position. My grandmother taught me how to crochet. Slip knot.
Having the amaranth yarn make the first hole is to open another hole
another hole another hole. Drops soldier to a chain at the long-lashed
eaves I don't carry a pail to. Carrying loss is to open loss like a
package: a snarl of yarn or a window you climb over when the bars fall
away, the room you hear the ill

-oiled swing of a sewing machine, the foot treadle groaning a rust-
ridden elegy. To be unable to search for my sea-glass quietude in the
red-oxide drone. The way the bamboo cane chairs my skin in time-
traceries. Drugged in desperation, the yarn breaststroking to safety—
there is a kind of wide-eyed safety in distance, or so the thought, in
moving away from initiality—*yarn over, yarn through, yarn over, yarn
through.* But the truth that moving away can only be moving closer.
Crocheting is

circling back to the first hole over and monsoon over. She taught me to
celebrate absence by creating a whorl around it. Chingam-Kanni-
Thulam-Vrischikam-Dhanu-Makaram-Kumbham-Meenam-Medam-
Edavam-Mithunam-Karkadakam.

* Chingam-Kanni-Thulam-Vrischikam-Dhanu-Makaram-Kumbham-
Meenam-Medam-Edavam-Mithunam-Karkadakam: months in
Malayalam calendar

Published in Posit, Issue 32, *January 2023*

RAMESH KARTHIK NAYAK
Tree

Grandmother said
trees are my ancestors.

If trees are my ancestors
then all elements on the earth
are proofs of my history.

I went hunting once
and took a nap
on the swollen root overground
where I had a dream —
a fog descended from sky,
a dust of seeds
that bloomed white flowers
in their fall,
oozing the spirit of life
chanting our ancestors' names.

I woke up
from a timeless nap,
felt the muscles
swollen over my skin.

I touched them —
there was a stream inside.
I heard
the rustling of leaves,
crackling of branches,
gusts of whistling winds.

I felt
my history is within me.

I should read my history
flowing in my veins.

Published in Chakmak, *Red River, August 2023*

RANJIT HOSKOTE
Bākhā

That wide unalloyed sky from which the rain
    would pour without question on a plateau where

the fort around which the people lived was called Fort
the language that they spoke was called Language
the script in which their letters flowed was called Hand
the people with the loudest voices were called High
the people whose voices they smothered were called Mute

Under that wide unalloyed sky where *Bākhā* was the name
they gave to the sweet speech that flowered in their songs of praise
and to the callused worker who drowned in the sludge of their drains

Published in Verseville, *Vol. XXXVI, December 2023*

RANU UNIYAL
Hard to Find

I am good
Amma holds her heart
inside her fist.

It is a cold *Sankranti* for her
and my only son
struggling with dysgraphia rattles
the mobile number of his father.

A lullaby whines and I see her
riding in the submissive dark
with eyes flipping at unknown bridges.

There is water everywhere
The sky is full of treasure
and the earth has returned all her dues.
To wind she had her smiles to offer,

wings, furs, tapioca, coconut shells
syllables, ragas, laughter, and stray wounds
there is enough to last a lifetime,

Till date nobody knows where she has stored that gift of fire.

Published in Borderless Journal, *January 2023*

RESHMA RUIA
The Weekend Life of My Mother

On Saturdays
Mother's lipsticked mouth is a boxing glove
One false move and she'll knock you down
A dragon tattoo curls down the side of her bicep
Her jeans are ripped knee to toe. She wheels her bike out in the sun
Sits astride whilst chewing fried chicken bun
Mother is 'Firecracker' to her friends
She bets on horses with a few men
Sometimes she brings them home

On Sundays
She strolls through the mall shoplifts a bauble or two
Wrapped and ribboned she gifts me these. Hairbands and books
We slurp noodles in the food court and ride the bus to the sea
Her eyes are rimmed in blue kohl.
Her kisses taste of Sriracha sauce and smoke
'I want to be like you, Ma,' I say, arms wrapped tight around her waist
'Don't you dare, 'she hisses but she's pleased I can tell

On Mondays
Mother gets up early. Changes two buses and goes to work in big grey
overalls that dwarf her limbs
Her hair pulled back- is a sparrow's tail.
Cheeks soap clean like a nun's
She nibbles her cheese sandwich on a park bench in her lunch break
And spends her day filing nails of women who call her
'Cindy 'and pat her shoulder when she pours them ginger tea

Published in Northern Gravy Issue Eight, *March 22, 2023*

RHITAMA BASAK

In the Language of Birds

I grew up feeding grains to crows
picking fallen feathers to hide 'em in the cupboard
matchstick homes for ants in the backyard
ants who came and left and never grew into a tree or a tiger with blue
eyes.

Crows interrupt you.
They always do. In warm countries
rain is almost always delayed
as you walk past
on Sundays by the red walls
newspapers strew the pavements down your window –
your *nazms** bleeding. Close it, do.

Crows interrupt you.

*"main ab kesaalparindokadinmanaunga
mere paas walejangal se baat ho gayi hai"*+

We read on.

I'll write to rain in the language of birds.
I'll write you in blue, grey,
in parrot green.
Olive, mauve and shades that you would never dream in, had you not
written (to) me.

The first thing I noticed away from home were skies without crows.
Skies that shone and rained and screamed
and never wrote to you.

I'll write again. I'll always do.
Forest air. Chewing gums
cooling your breath in the traffic of cities I've only met in delirious
khwaab**!

We die a little with every crow that's caught in storm!
With each thunder, we die a little
on *Shab-e-Qadr****
I'll write again, *Sham-e-Ummeed****!*
I'll write to you in the language of birds.

Published in Muse India, Issue 107, *Jan-Feb 2023*

RISHI DASTIDAR
Peace

A used lance becomes a needle.
Chain mail as silver cotton thread.
Stitched into the murmuring breeze,
White eagles asleep, wings unspread.

Published in Setu Magazine, *April 2023*

ROCHELLE POTKAR
Confluence

Waters when they evaporate, meet…
at a global conference, to speak of fish dropouts,
obscura of clouds, near-deaths, hydrological dynamics,
monocultures, and metals:
nickel, lead, chromium, at their beds.
The bend is notional: water for coffee, cane,
banana, paddy,
mills, distilleries,
fertilizerplants.
The Aral Sea was water for cotton
in Uzbekistan:
one shirt drinking 2000 liters,
now more saline than the Dead Sea –
palm-sized, a fossil-tiger's footprint,
plains of salt, toxic dust storms,
fishing towns, now ship-graveyards.
people, sick; dumps of pathogenic weapons
making the summers hotter, winters colder,
the Aral Sea is the Aralkum desert.

And if seas made maps,
rivers, homes
men, borders.

The Cauvery too is uprising
         – one of the longest-running rivers
over her water share to ripple greens
for Karnataka and Tamil Nadu,
when her sand beds expand for mining
flowing from Brahmagiri

on her way to the Bay of Bengal,
she worries if those warring over her understand
that a river is a person,
like Whanganui of New Zealand
– ancestor of 160 years
that got legal status
through the longest-running litigation
by the Māori people
because mountains too
are equal to men.

Published in Greening the Earth, Penguin Anthology, *29 May 2023*

RUTH VANITA
Almas Ali Khan, Khwajasarai, died 1808

'The best and greatest man in Awadh – '
so said Sleeman, who rarely praised an Indian.
Wealthier than the king, and yet a slave,
Haryana boy, part of a queen's dowry,
castrated convert, he learnt the courtly arts,
guarded treasures, rose to rule a realm –
'The whole country in his charge a garden'.

Slaves have no heirs, queens cannot trust their sons –
the king awaits his death, and Hastings plots it
but he remained the queen's faithful ally,
survived starvation, fetters, torture.
Twenty years later, six feet tall, and stout,
'A venerable being, upwards of eighty'.

Death near, he took his papers to the mosque,
there threw them in the tank – records of loans
to the region's noblemen and rulers;
forgave all debts, gave to the poor, to poets,
leaving little for the king to seize. Twenty years

more, only the legend lingered
among the Awadhi peasants he called children;
and temples, tanks, mosques, forts, hospitals.
His nephew, Raja Bhagmal, built at Phaphund
a mosque that bears his name and Shah Jafar's.
There a sage lived, his friend Mahant Sahajanand.

Pity him not, whose wrongs, a world away,
caused Burke to rage in pain and grief, whose death,
Insha, the elegant, the witty,
mourned, 'Alas, Alas, I mourn Almas'.
Almas – a diamond that cannot be cut.

Published in The Broken Rainbow, *Copper Coin, 2023*

SAHANA AHMED
Dolls for Muslim Girls

Barbie can be a mother,
and a good Muslim,
married to a Salim / Saad / Sa'id, if we hold her near a flame
till her face disappears.

Dolls that look like humans,
with lips, eyes, brows, and teeth,
are haram.
Islam is not a part-time faith.

As for Peppa,
Winnie, Minnie, et cetera —
one should cut off their heads. There is nothing wrong with that.

Published in Usawa Literary Review, *June 2023*

SAIMA AFREEN
Winter Biomythography

-    *Enroute to Chicago*
is etched on the back of a train caterpillaring
towards fog that grazes the cloche hats of Hopper's
girls. Above, Orion's watch; his light varnishes
my infernal heart, its mouth

open for a small dose of snowflakes that leave
their lacy prints ahead of the iron wheels,   ahead
of the monstrous weight of what remains unfinished
in long white smudges like a snowed-in sea returning
the debt it owes to the land. Underneath, a thousand
poets sleep with their songs on infinite possibilities
of betrayal. Of setting your own heart on fire. Smell
the perfume, feel its droplets on your lips and recite
a prayer for this body, this scented heart(h). All this
while cupping this white fur of a city.

Published in chapbook Winter Biomythography, *Press 254, US,*
December 2023.

SAMBHU R
Well

My mother draws water from the well
that has been dreaming in our courtyard
for three generations. She balances
herself on a mouldering wooden crate
in which a distant uncle from Ooty
once sent sweet plums on a whim.
Her anklets tinkle against the long grass
where kraits hide their supreme indifference
to human fate. She lowers the pail
with a premonitory quiver into the entrails
of the cool creamy water blistered
by somnolent striders, overcoming one fear
at a time. The pail clinks timorously
as the rope jerks, and my mother holds
her breath to let the wind uncoil
from her wrists. The loupe-wearing eye
of the well zooms in on the clock hands
clashing on the dial of her face.
The surface parts. Striders relocate.
With a soft tugging motion
mother resurrects the drowned pail
out of the well of her existence,
its heaviness returning like memory.
The thirst burning on her thin lips
has learnt to wait. She must now
pour herself out till the last drop for others.

Published in Setu, *December 2023*

SANGITA KALARICKAL
Good Touch, Bad Touch

The water flows down her hair, her face, and her bare back, neem soap suds mingling with her silent tears. For a long time, she scrubs herself until the normally gleaming brown skin looks bruised, raw, and red. The lather flows through a blurry haze in a thin stream toward the drain.

A burst of metallic taste springs in her mouth as she bites her palm hard. The wail should never escape her throat. It would never do if the rest of the family hears.

temple hall steps
the stain of marigolds
crushed underfoot

Published in haikuKATHA *Issue 26, December 2023*

SANJEEV SETHI
Fluidities

In last night's clasp, mirrors that shy away from me crack
open. Boundaries are laid bare on the playground of
the persuasive or the potent. You keep your thigh away;
I hide a part of myself from yours truly. In our eatery,
no one identifies with hunger.

The universe speaks in a voice of its own. Poetry permits us
to cross the confines without penalties: Some are rigid or
too right to do otherwise. In silence, we learn the alphabet;
stillness helps discover the diction. When we are ready,
the conversation begins.

Published in Otoliths, *Australia, Issue 69, May 1, 2023*

SANJUKTA DAS GUPTA
Shikhandi

Who am I
What am I
My father Dhrupada
Wanted a son
Obediently I became a son
I had a wife who
Screamed her top off
When she saw I was a woman

Then when all of them
Were no match for Bhisma
Tricks were the only way
Stooping to conquer
A part of any war-game

Neither a son, nor a daughter
I was the one on exhibit
Appalled elderly Bhisma
Laid down his arms
Lay on a bed of spears

Sighting me Bhisma's resolve
Not to fight a woman
Half or full
Led to his end
As the Pandavas cheered.

No one inquired what happened
To me after the great war was fought
Won by some, lost by many.
In fact, I was sliced in two

That Great Indian story
Is awash with blood, sweat and tears
Fratricide, killing of kin
Deception, gambling, disguise
Confidence trickery
I am just a footnote
An user-friendly
Not quite non-binary.

Published in Ekalavya Speaks*, Kolkata Penprints, 2023*

SARABJEET GARCHA
Return

A woman
carrying a diya
in a glass-and-iron case
from her kitchen to the riverside samadhi
of her patron   a scholar who left no books behind
doesn't want to imagine what roads death takes

all she wants this moment is to shield the wicklight
from the evening's erratic breath

the stone temple on the far bank sways
to the melody of a bhajan   the deity has vanished

someone
who couldn't stay indoors
who is now close to leaning over the water's edge
to wash away the day's contaminants

spots a firefly across the river   a drop of varnish
                        on black fabric
and senses the missing
                          approaching

First published in All We Have, *Kolkata: Chair Poetry Books,*
November 2023

SARANYA SUBRAMANIAN
Navratri on the Muni

tired of rejecting your temporary home (denial is serious work), you
stretch your arms wide and embrace the fog, stop the 31, and accept
that you are eating a bagel and drinking a coffee. no milk. the blasphemy.

yes, this is temporary, and yes, you shouldn't be here, and yes, you came
here just to leave, but you are here now, and it is navratri, a new year,
and you are still here. and exhausted after rejecting yet another

temporary life, you turn the blue muni seats into a kovil of your own:
a kovil in transit— *things standing shall fall, but the moving ever shall stay*
— and realise that basavanna was writing for you. way before there were

buses and aeroplanes and nation states and passports and visas and
immigration, he was writing for you. his poetry stands for you. And
even though you are far from home, the distance is unable to take

your prayer away: the one you say every time you feel alone. Which
has happened in every city you have stepped into, every new identity
you have created— *my legs are pillars/ the body the shrine/ the head*

a cupola/ of gold— every place of worship you've built in transit. today,
bagel and coffee in hand, you mutter all 108 names from the durga ashtothram
inside this makeshift munikovil, and suddenly you remember

doing this on the mumbai local, the delhi metro, the bengaluru metro, the
sonipat shuttle, the chennai mtc, the bombay best, the zurich sbb, the
london tube, the vancouver translink. you remember the same restlessness,

the same frustration of not having reached, of waiting to get home, of never
really being at home for some fucking reason, and you sing out in sorrow
at how surreal this all has been so far, you sing out in exasperation, you sing

out the same song every, every time— என்னகவிபாடினாலும், உந்தன்மனம் இரங்கவில்லை— you sing out, you sing to muruga, muruga, can you hear me, can you hear me calling you, can you see me in this muni, can you bring me home

Published in The Bombay Literary Magazine, *April 2023*

SARASWATI NAGPAL
January Hymn

Another year of thirteen moons. Hawks skim
foam on leaves of dawn, a surfer dives, carmine
board flung up by wave, then swallowed. All is
drowned in ocean roar.

I have shadows where your voice nestled
in me. Long, like ancient kelp leaves
lingering in troubled tides.

Time rolls on, washes up iterations of me:
driftwood, seaweed, unborn dreams
wrack line of what could have been
strewn in nameless knots.

Yet some pearl of who I was to you
endures unravaged by living debris
lucid in dappled silence, love-washed grief.

A migration of crabs hails sunrise with wide
arms and slanted crawl. Seagulls ascend. Far, far
the glint of dolphins reverent upon lapis sea.

Published in *Atlanta Review, Fall/Winter 2023*

SEKHAR BANERJEE
The Roll Call

A prayer is not silence. It is a housing, bombed several times.
You do roll call
of all friends and relatives
in the long nights of December. You enter your sleep
wearing a grey coat,
carrying a notebook and a pomegranate
every night. Each seed is for a departed relative
while the play field across the street
is covered with blue geraniums and weeds.

Published in Arkana: Issue 14/ June, 2023

SHANTA ACHARYA
Find Me

In a child refugee's orphaned eyes, find me.
In the daily promise of sunrise, find me.

Soldiers rescue an old woman, a bag of bones
trapped in rubble, calling out to the skies: *Find me.*

Women and children disappear without a trace.
In their helpless, anguished cries, find me.

Surveying the desolation of ruined lives
in forsaken cities of grief the wind sighs, find me.

In voices rising from shallow graves, souls cry,
emerging like a flutter of butterflies, find me.

Unheard, unrepresented, they survive like seeds
praying in cracks of abandoned high-rise, find me.

In stories buried in the bones of exiles,
forgotten in the annals of history's lies, find me.

Published in the Journal of Postcolonial Writing, *Vol 59, No 2, April 2023*

SHANTANU RAY CHAUDHURI
Ghazal: Tonight

I think I will let it all be tonight
Stop thinking and be free tonight

All creation is fleeting, a play of illusion
I too cease looking for eternity tonight

Straddling the eras I stand, Time incarnate
Past, present and future rise within me tonight

How petty my concerns, trivial all pursuit seem
When in you, God at play I see tonight

The many hurt I cause the people I love
Seeps into my heart to haunt me tonight

Whose divine voice is it that comes riding?
The breeze that caresses the trees tonight

What can I ever offer you, eternal stranger?
But these words that ring empty tonight

Words are all I have, my genesis, my end
And these words will set me free tonight

Why not cast the dark from your soul, Sahar
And lose yourself forever in the light tonight

Published in *Undiscovered Journal*, 5 July 2023

SHAURYA PATHANIA
The Right Choice

Money and mother rarely settled with each other,
She never liked riches. She never saw it too.

When I planned to leave my home for a city,
She cursed at me for choosing money over her,

I wanted to tell her it was for her well-being.
A case of convenience begins there.

She listed all the perks of a rural household,
My capitalist comforts fell short in the argument
(But has an argument ever been just)

I won against ma, she cried on it
With a hand over my head and holding me to her chest.

I visit her once in a while,
She denies all my gifts and when I return,
She still cries.

In order to know that Ma was and will always be right,
I keep her photograph in my wallet.

Published in Riot Ghoul Print Magazine, *September 2023*

SHELLY BHOIL
Unpretentious Things

what about surrendering yourself to unpretentious
things like the chair in the corner that invites you to
sit down and lean on its back when you are tired.
look at that gape-mouthed spoon and the pot-bellied glass
thirsting for your touch. even the palms of your hands tend
to cup into the well of blessing for you. and, wow, what's more
promising than the sun behind the curtain in your window.
it's peeping in and almost touching your toe. there is wood too
on the hearth to warm you. the generosity of broken things is
almost always unconditional. they give to you beyond themselves. and
this is why i am given to believing that the world is not half bad
in moments of someone saying to someone 'you can do it',
'i am happy for you', 'it will get better'

Published in The Brooklyn Rail, *April 2023*

SHIKHA MALAVIYA
The Meen Woman
not a mean woman, but one who is all *Meen &Akshi,* glassy fish eyes
that see everything, whose hands are all scale, fins and guts,
as she sits on her haunches in front of her basket
a thimble of today's ocean spread out, tails up
her polyester saree
is printed palm fronds pleated with
the scent of salt, sand
and the day's humidity
don't let the rope
of jasmine pinned to her hair
fool you
one whiff of her
drags you to the bottom
of the Mariana trench
and to stand next to her
means interoceanic travel
hanging onto a sperm whale's tail
the *meen* woman smiles
a mouth full of shark teeth
stained with the blood
of areca nut
wrapping today's catch
in day old newspaper
your money tucked
between her breasts
as you wonder how
it might feel to
touch her
the
ache like a
fishbone
caught
in your
throat

Published in Pratik Magazine, *January 2023*

SHIKHANDIN
Kathali Champa

My mother's history excluded me.
But it wasn't all bad. There were bits
and bobs of pity, kindness tossed
like old bread to a starving street dog.
Now they dot my mind.
Fugitive stars on a moon-bright night.
Green-white was the colour of her favourite flower,
turned waxy yellow when ripe with perfume.
It hid itself among the leaves, letting its secret out
only through its jackfruit-scent in the gloaming.
I caught the heady whiff, and lapped it up
like a thirsty but alert rodent before the shattered jug.
That flower never bloomed for me. It never knew me.
I knew it though, like I knew the distant sun.

A strand of sunlight combs my salt-pepper hair.
I close my eyes and reach out for a pair
of hands. My heart inhales from its cup.
The bustle of academia fans the air.
Nothing remotely floral here. Except for this
tenderness. This ease of ownership.
Stolen flower-scent fades into mist.
"Let go," the hands say. "Let go. Let go."

A helium-filled balloon lifts, and disappears
into the deepening blue. The evening star
gives me its unblinking stare. The bell-chime
of a now grown-up child's laughter settles
around me like a doll's crinoline skirt.
The dust of the past blows away

like smoke through the window.
All is quiet and in repose, except
for the coiling fragrance of a flower
clotting into a bead of blood in my heart.

Published in The EKL Review, *April 2023*

SHILPA DIKSHIT THAPLIYAL
Thresholds of Summer

What vault of memories lies open at the threshold of every summer?
Rusty decades, they hesitate over thresholds, every summer.

Silver anklets rustling in the wind, scent of patchouli on warm skin,
we sauntered through aisles of chinars, blooms of marigolds that
　　　summer.

Boatmen on shikaras, with songs on lips, trinkets of floating markets,
liquid dawn drenches, the Dal Lake beckons, beholds every summer.

In the valleys of Gulmarg, potatoes in clay fire, saffron in hot tea:
pitchers of pilfered moments decanted into these pot-holed summers.

Dusty floors, bare walled, empty home. What day is it today?
Unread mail, sliced apples, your forehead, ice-cold, one summer.

Echo of conch, temple bells; lamps burning on parapets.
Pallbearers, angels, descend on a household in summer.

Melon moon parked over portico; Lata, Mukesh hum on radio.
In converging umbras, sketches in sepia unfold every summer.

The empty muslin bedsheet, long nights pinned on terraces. Inch by
　　　inch,
I scout for your fingertips, your smile, to steer through these blindfolds
　　　of summer.

In red paisleys and whorls of dahlias, I cross-stitch eternityin threads of gold. In standstill of scarlet dawn, I spread them four folds every
summer.

Musty bookshelves, sheaves of dog-eared papers. *Srinagar '70,* says ink in blue. *O heart, how unprepared are you?* This chokehold, every
summer.

Published in PR&TA Issue 3, Encounters And Entanglements, *28 August 2023*

SHOBHANA KUMAR

Picture Perfect

You both lie asleep with heads buried inside down-feather quilts. You are here but, in your dreams, you are in another world. I look at your faces for a long time, marvelling at how beautifully life has planted her blessings on you. In your eyes, there are a million visions waiting to unfold. In your ears, sounds of the world wait to arrive and find their way into your soul. On your faces, the angels dance songs of peace and love.

cuckoo calls
a long-forgotten story
emerges in the mind

I look at your tiny limbs and wonder how far you will walk with them. What will you make with your hands? For whom will your heart beat and skip one? In how many ways will you feed your soul and mind?

monsoon
      morning paw prints
in the foyer

Published in The Wise Owl, *April 2023*

SHRUTI SAREEN
Romancing the Oleander

I desired its pink flowers
and its spiky, lance-like leaves.
I read one could get you poisoned
and twelve could leave you dead.
The yellow flowers are the commonest
in India, but the red, being more poisonous
would suit my purpose better. The seeds
would do just as well. Anything, really.
Any part of this pretty ornamental garden plant
which hid death in the whorls of its flowers.
How harsh a death could such a pretty flower
bring, after all, and such a lilting flower name
though the leaves are bitter? The flowers too,
 I suppose. Imagine a pretty death
devoid of bitterness. They sell a plant for about
three hundred rupees, on Amazon. I thought
I could keep a plant-pet, love it, grow it,
 perhaps eat it. I could always garden,
in case I didn't die. Thus I have a macabre romance
with the oleander. Either I grow the oleander,
or the oleander kills me.

Published in Panocha Zine, *USA, Issue 10, July 2023*

SHYAMASRI MAJI
Healing

Not an eye for an eye,
but, a grove of palm trees
bracing the silver mirage
to recall what happened between us

A speck was it or was it the cricket-calling moon
we viewed from the bivouac of imagined love?
Our shadows spoke their own tongue.
You clicked on the 'skip' option.

The night froze into a macular dot.
Pain hardened here and there
on the igneous slopes
like clots of blood in the murder spot,
like dewdrops on the rowdy splinters

The winter arrived and departed
the brown crust fell off the wound.
I saw you anew:
A healed scar you are,
an indelible white on my dark skin

Published in Outlook India Weekender, *11 March, 2023*

SIDDHARTH DASGUPTA
A Swimmer in the Tropics

Azaan already. Birds fill the sky in a dress
rehearsal for their tropical longing.
I was at the Cobbler most of last night,
drinking martinis filled with the temptation
of distant lands. We're not so dissimilar
you know, the birds and I—just creatures
fed by the pull of their separable tropical
elsewheres. Azaan already, and the city
is prayer. Belief and unbelonging.
I stopped reading the newspaper
sometime in 2003. It keeps piling up like
residual afterburn—the hatred,
the glorification of bad; the bare bones
of countries with no conception of dry
land. Azaan already. Deliver me,
o ghosts of Rafi Sahab and Nusrat Sahab,
o ghosts of Geeta Dutt and Runa Laila.
Keep me pure and hopeful for this world.
Keep me alive to the tides that prosper
like foreordained stories. Some days,
I wish this city had a sea. But,
it's azaan already. Some days, I think that
city is just another word for drowning.

Published in The Common, *October 2023*

SIVAKAMI VELLIANGIRI
Idioms and Phrases

I remember the two notebooks Appa
slipped into my pinafore pockets, one for adamant
spelling, the other for phrases and idioms.
'Don't try to pull my legs', is not the same as
pulling the teeth, so I turn to Sushruta—
I learn about ancient Ayurveda, about physicians
being poets first, how they watched the heads of birds
to make dog-faced, tiger faced, wolf faced, bear faced,
hyena faced, lion faced, crow faced, heron faced
forceps, how hammer, bone-saw, scalpel, nail-puller
lancet, sharp probe, tooth scaler (full caps) scissors,
sharp hook, awl, trocar, circular knife,
single edged knife, chisel, not to speak
of the suturing needle (they used ants for this,
live ants.)

'Instruments were imagined for real pain.'

I kill my darlings, the cartoon of a calf elephant
pulling a string tied to a patient's tooth,
and falling on its back.

Published in Free-the-Verse, *Summer 2023*

SONI SOMARAJAN
Everest

The submersibles descend. We watch our breaths
dissipate in a plume, a release unto the aqueous light.
A scatter of sunfire floats on the surface, the semester's
most anticipated day. Above, our home ships rest,
drinking from their solar sails—a respite from roving
earth's watery face. We slip slowly but don't go
too far, just fifty fathoms deep into the bleak ink.
And we see it rising, a peak no longer clad in snow,
unlike the pictures from the class presentation.

Like suspended dugongs, the five submersibles
surround the summit, solemnly as if it were a ritual,
silencing a brief burst of instinctive applause.
On cue, someone turns off the lights within,
the radio's chatter. The teacher signals us to survey
what the headlights expose—the bird's eye view.
But we aren't silent. Like a sacred spell, our minds
mutter a prayer she holds forth in every lesson:
see the bigger picture, see the bigger picture.

Published in Count Every Breath: A Climate Anthology, *May 14, 2023*

SONNET MONDAL
The Trident and the Tea-Seller

The trident lightning arrestor
looks more constant than before—

besieged by discomfort,
bygone joys and pain—a belief
flowing endlessly into the future.

The creepers cannot
offer love to it—no red or yellow flowers.

The tea-seller beside the closed factory
never noticed it since the trident
didn't ever arrest or spear any lightning

especially when the radical flags
were offering a yearlong monsoon
to a sneaking venomous rust.

There is now a vacuum inside the gates,
patches of love and strife on the trident
and outside some tea for passers-by.

Published in Indian Literature *journal IL 334, 2023*

SOPHIA NAZ
Night of the Mosquito

I am body, lonely prey
You, a wave, warrior tribe.

We are a battle fought
night after night on

porous borders, sound
of one hand slapping

sleepless grounds, worn out -
posts of sheets where blood -

sucking toes the line.
Majoritarian *macchar** versus

embattled *khatmal,** I am
hounded by sirens, marooned

by yet another dig, in
what's left over of my skin.

*macchar (mosquito) and *khatmal* (bedbug) are slang for Sunni and Shia

Published in Usawa Literary Review, *Issue 9, May-June 2023*

SUCHI GOVINDARAJAN
Dead Tree

Instead of mourning, watch
how lichen blooms lace
on my old and storied limbs,
            how aphids gather for feasts.
Remember the storm that opened
            a fissure?
Some bats, they darken leather there
and in the day, while they sleep,
            each inside their closed umbrellas,
a small and tailless coppersmith bird
stops and calls
            and calls to dissolve your sorrow,
taps me to find the portholes
I have hidden away for lovers.

Published in the Sound and Vision edition, Black Bough Poetry, *April 2023*

SUDEEP SEN
Language

*Without translation, I would be limited to the borders of
my own country. The translator is my most important ally.*
— Italo Calvino

My typewriter is multilingual,
its keys mysteriously calibrating

my bipolar, forked tongue.
Black-red silk ribbon spools, unwinds

as the carriage moves right to left.
In cursive hand, I write from left to right.

My tongue was born promiscuous —
speaking in many languages.

My heart spoke another, my head
yet another — the translation, seamless.

*

Auricles, ventricles pump blood —
corpuscle-like alphabets, phrases, syntax

cross-fertilize my text, breathing life.
Texture enriched — music, cadence

spatially enhanced — osmotic,
polyglottal — a polygamy of grammar.

Letterforms dance, ligatures pirouette —
ascenders, descenders — pitch perfect.

Imagination isn't caged in speech —
speech cannot be caged in language.

Published in Textus, *Issue 7, 2023*

SUHIT BOMBAYWALA
Ghazal- "I drank the city..."

I drank the city and fell silent.
As the stupor left me, I became a poet.

A knife in bloom is a harmless evil.
A blade of grass can maim a poet.

Scrivener, take refuge in your wounds.
Moon-junkie: what else to name a poet?

Keep in escrow the proceeds of sorrow.
Who's not seduced by fame? A poet.

Make the crystal shape itself, Suhit.
Be water-pure as a gem, a poet.

Published in Saarangaa, *15th June, 2023*

SUNIL RAJAGOPAL
Upriver

Rain is like love, an unexpected guest knocking at windows. Waking you from daily life, asking you to open your eyes and dream. It lies over the land like a warm, wet blanket. A weeping cloud, right on the road. Not a moment back, a Great Hornbill passed. Yellow casque and pied wings clumsy, in the drop laden quiet.

Every drop adds to the river on a pilgrimage. The river is in flood, not far away. The road is high, floating on water. The water is high, taller than elephant grass. Great arcing buffalo horns sail upriver, past islands overgrown with clunky pachyderms.

The river is like love. Deeper, broader, year after year; a ritual of mud and ruin. It brings you gifts but slits you open to take things away unasked. Upriver, it carves through gorges. Here it swallows fields and forest, boats and rhinos. And when it has left, only scars remain. Red vertiginous walls with slivers of metal and hard rock. Plains drowning in silt and debris. Death, with a promise of fertility.

The river is like love. If it floods for long enough, it will wash us away and leave what is needed behind.

Published: "When Ants Grow Wings", *Authorspress, August 2023*

SUNIL SHARMA
Associations

The gentle wind
reminds

the female immigrant
of

a Margo tree
in

the courtyard of a
two-storied home
in Greater Noida, kissed

by
a crimson sun; a tree with stories
and teen secrets
hanging from its boughs
and leaves.

The smell
of the grassy grounds

sweetened
by the summer
rain in Toronto

brings back the smells
of

the soil in the flower-beds
and front garden,
forever enshrined in the mind.

Published in The Chakkar, *October 9, 2023*

TABISH NAWAZ
Hypnagogia

The lake dries up,
turns into a cage, reflects
the sky within the ruin of water.
Every night a moon ferments sadness
into an essence of camphor,
squinting across the doorway
of the days spent in exile.
The birds of rainbow
fly away, leaving behind flakes
of memories, sticking like soot
along the wall. A finger leaps on,
staring, a fable of footprints forms,
and fades beneath the lamp,
weeping itself to darkness.
An arrow goes round and round
waking up the hours
from the belly of time.

Published in Jaden Magazine *(UK), Issue 5, July 2023*

TANSY TROY
Silent Conversation

Outside the bookshop in which I first held you
(*The Friend*, says Hafiz, *is both far and near*),
founded just after Partition
split us all,
until we chose rebirth,
making and mending,
tying up odd karmic ends,
completing narratives
before extinction,

I stop: standing on the threshold.

Once within, I comprehend
how Time is, yet cannot be.

For if you too have stepped into this hallowed space,
then you are stepping still;
and when you walk past that cheery pot
of riotous yellow chrysanthemums,
or invite the passing chai walla
to pour you out a cup,
you too may feel my shadow here, as I feel yours.

Head bowed over book in prayer:
ghost *lecteur*, you observe
me reading the many yous
on every printed page.

Published in Hindustan Times, *December 2023*

TASEER GUJRAL
Ceremony

Draw the curtains please
Set the table for two
I look out from fogged windows
and wait with all my might
(the only thing I do well)
Every fallen leaf is a sign
Of ever same days ahead
The earth will not stop spinning
The earth will always speak
the same language
The fork clanks against the cold china
I look out and notice
An orange sunslanting
along the horizon, and
Though the lime continues to shed leaves
A stillness hangs in the air
In my thoughts I see your shadow
Etched against the glass
lighting a cigarette,
I let the memories dissolve
Washed in relief
That you will never be home

Published in From My Window Anthology, *30 June 2023*

TASNEEM KHAN
Imperfect Refugee: A Ghazal

Belas in her rings, O Yasmeen! You become a flower–blooming in
    translation
I say–beautiful, pretty–A tongue exiled: *Mallika-e-bahaar* receding in
    translation

"*Insha 'Allah* this war will end"? Before *Ka 'aba*, she prostrates on red
    anemones
A God expelled from the edge of a prayer–holy grief–weeping in
    translation

A finger halts at *waqf-e-taam*–In its womb remains–Prisoner of a
    language lost
Damned hands turn to stone–A believer's faith*less* heart, bleeding in
    translation

Zaynab's lament ends in Damascus, Now who is left to weep for the
    mourners?
An ancient sorrow–A threshold of words–A *Truth* festering in
    translation

Language's imperfect refugee–I pray in Arabic, Grieve in Urdu,
    Protest in Silence
I, Ana–This ghazal's criminal, arrive in English, now watch me–
    collapsing in translation

Note:
Waqf-e-taam- It means 'the perfect stop 'in Arabic. *Waqf* implies 'stop. '
It refers to the finishing of a specific verse in The Quran, meaning for the
reader to stop and reflect. There are various other types of *waqfs* as well.

Published in PostScript, *English Literary Society, St. Stephen 's College,*
14 December, 2023

TEJASWINEE ROYCHOWDHURY
How My Mother Brought Back Lights this Diwali

Last year, when my father let in the darkest night
mum vowed to eat all 12 *purnima* moons
so their lights would spill out of her
in the shape of little fairies
purple and green.

Published by Black Bough Poetry *in the Christmas-Winter Anthology,*
Volume 4 on 26 November 2023

TEJI SETHI
Haibun

it is

breast
lesion
the
contorted
margins
of
a
lie

my eyes fixed
on the mammogram
thoughts wander

fading
noon
an
incision
invades
my
silence

surgeon's office
slides mounted with
traces of denial

his
pen
moves
the
elegant
curve
of
C

Published in Muse India, *Vasant Ritu – Spring Special Issue No. 108,*
June 2023

UMA GOWRISHANKAR
Four Ragam

Kanakangi
She knows from the jaggery melting in the uruli,
it is a girl. The tidal wave washes in the dream,
the demoness shapes cell upon cell and the light dances
on the string of lamps in the temple as she glides fistful
of radiance in the uncut gems at her throat—the gold
smelts serration of syllables into vortices of notes.

Ratnangi
In the clearing sequestered beyond the tall grass stalks,
she polishes the secrets of the breeze in the stones;
the red earth stains her feet and soaks into her nails,
the crimson blush as if the heart bleeds when the cornea
explodes like gemstones with a hundred wrinkles in the faces
of women who toss black and red grains into the lake.

Gnanamurti
She could not help it, the wings flexing and the levitating,
the earth slipping away, the waves lapping, gurgling,
its speech like a child's: soft rumbles of joy tuned
in perfection to the formation of geese tearing the sky
in a sweep like the whirring wipers arcing again
and again to uncover the face behind the misted glass.

Vakulabaranam

From the bottomless silence of the river, the currents eddy
in a helix of rapture when her fingers rifle the blue lotus
that clouds from the swirl of her voice ascending to grasp
the pollens exploding from the crown of vakula flowers—
crescents of moon woven in strands browned with undying
fragrance on her skin blue-greened from his touch.

Published in Feral: A Journal of Poetry and Art, *Issue 16, June 30, 2023*

URNA BOSE
Why a Peace Poem Must Die

The peacock must have its mating dance,
the Gulmohar, its red, hot rage.
Honesty must have its tail tucked
between its hind legs, crouched
behind the trembling bush.
Lest fate gets handed out nimbly: a deer
caught in the headlights - ready for the clicking
cameras of a hoard of spectator-sport tourists.

Pink-plumaged flamingos crash landing on an
indolent swamp, a reminder that seasons are
caravans as are politicians, cultivated points of view,
and elaborately drawn-up party manifestos.
That blood-plumaged wars cannot be left behind
in the pages of a yellowed history textbook,
priced Rs 210, moth-eaten in a rickety stall
in College Street, Kolkata.

And, the reason why a peace poem cannot hoist
a white flag on its whimpering chest,
the blaze breaking through the pores of its skin,
is only because its voice will be gagged,
its throat cut out in fine, fleshy juliennes,
at the phantom hour of its publication.

Published in Setu Journal, *Pittsburgh, USA, November 2023*

VIDYA SHANKAR
Mukha Lepham

Though uncomfortable, I wear a surgical mask whenever I go out.

    clipped wings

No one stares at me. But they would if I didn't wear one.

    all those pictures

The mask hides my distorted right cheek and scarred left chin—cruel reminders of the cancers that afflicted me.

    of flawless looks

*Mukha Lepham is an Ayurvedic anti-blemish face treatment.

Published in: haikuKATHA, *Issue 24, October 2023*

VIVEK SHARMA
A Sequestered Westerner

Should I describe myself in America as an Eastern Westerner?
Is it melanin or genes that make me a sequestered Westerner?

Baby suckled Eastern air, but also said: "Ne'er twain shall meet"
Ape Kipling, forget my *East* -- behave like that bastard Westerner?

Americans index a life's quality with the mortgage interest rates.
Seek an insomniac luxury to turn into a flustered Westerner?

Traffic tantrums, dust-storm Junes, mosquitoes, monsoon roads,
For me that *chaos makes sense*, I am not no dastard Westerner!

Deli sandwiches, deep-dish pizzas, Buffalo wings, pub burgers–
Can't swallow, can't relish, I remain a spicy-mustard Westerner!

Grammar of choices flatter with 24/7 AC-water-power-security.
Yet I ache for the *desi* ordeals; ain't I am an absurd Westerner?

Rushdie claims we are all migrants, from our territories or pasts.
What if my nostalgia is the optimism of an disinterred Westerner?

Whenever I visit India, callous comparisons engage my every step.
Am I embarrassed of my roots, am I now an awkward Westerner?

I live in the West, ever pine for the East: I await what epiphany?
Does the glory-ghoul tempt me to return as a conferred Westerner?

Jazz, Disney fables, turkey feasts, pumpkin ghosts, Coke's Santa Claus!
Don't I faithlessly adopt rituals to pass off as a die-hard Westerner?

Always ambushed by memories, as if, in East is my unfulfilled love.
Why not divorce my *Amrikidream-life* of a cloistered Westerner?

My creativity may flourish or famish in my East of parochial values.
Will my Eastern mother-tongue forgive this blustered Westerner?

O disciple of dueling heritages – is *Kavi* / Vivek Eastern or a Westerner?
Maybe an either / neither: dervish / bum, an erred/deferred Westerner.

Published in Muse India, *July-Aug 2023*

YAMINI DAND SHAH
Capitalising on Peace

Outskirts of Hyderabad witnesses farmer's two last suppers,
With Chinese insurgency tugging at seams of Itanagar,
As Dispur's eroding rain gauge,
Moulds casteist castings of ABC in Patna,
Sketching malnourished Bastar art adorning walls of museum in Raipur,
Mining away Panaji's frothy shores,
Therapying Gandhinagar's communal-industrial scorching,
Flaying floating fallen females adrift from doubly drugged Chandigarh,
Through sliding lands holding Shimla together,
Marking tribal statistics and parabolas of Ranchi,
Sowing debts reaping 'Bengalure',
As Thiruvananthapuram builds blocks of catastrophe,
While Bhopal is still a tragedy,
Reserving seats in an overrun Mumbai local,
Bordering insurgence 'Imphatically',
As we Journey along in deforested Shillong,
Having fragile roots below Aizawl,
Comprising of coarse ethnicities in memoriam at Kohima,
As walking skeletal bodies outside Bhubaneswar musea,
Blame silicosis for a child widower in Jaipur,
Although organic unemployment stares at Gangtok's whitewalls,
Just as language imposition gets scripted in Chennai,
Agartala's unmapped geographical isolation,
Makes Migrating away to try your Luck now,
In Dehradun's winding tour,
Waving a red flag on Kolkata's hand-pulled rickshaw,

An Indian exercise in capitalizing on peace
always excluding union territories.

Published in Peace through Poetry *Anthology, Adroit publishers 2023*

YUYUTSU SHARMA
On a Long-quarantined Night

Late into the night
you didn't return

as promised;
I longed for the sound

of your footfalls
on the creaking stairs

of our house
by the raging brook

and in the early
hours of the dawn

dreamt of a lush
grape-looking

new born
lying next to me,

your gift
at the dead end

of my long
quarantined night.

Published in The Brownstone Annual Anthology, *1st March, 2023*

ZAINAB WAHAB
The Terror of Small Things

They won't come near you.
All the small and slimy things
Are more afraid of you
Than you are of them
They said.

Look, how the roaches scuttle into darkness
To escape the threat of shadows
The spiders detangle from their webs
And the lizards crawl back into the highest shelves.

Child, look, how small in front of you.

Small, meaning harmless
Meaning they will die easy
Meaning they will perish without turning
Your memory into a crime scene.

We learn to live with the small things
Because we can kill them anytime.

And nothing
Prepares us for the terror
Of a small thing
Staring back.

Published in Gulmohur Quarterly, *29 December 2023*

ZILKA JOSEPH
For the Big Brown Bat

--The generic name Eptesicus is derived from the Greek, meaning "house flyer".

House flyer. Perhaps you have made your home
here. Like us, you stay. Perhaps you have found
that small hole to get inside and you dove
in again. This time when we were awake,
on a fun Friday night, when drinking wine,
watching TV, we saw you! I've wondered
if the slats on the deck is your day time
hang out. You've wormed your way to our garage,
or laundry room? Or a vent? A mystery
we must solve. For now, I shall look for trails
of scat. Little turds. Smell of ammonia
near the furnace, sniff hard around sump pump,
shelves. You can't hide. The spirits who dwell here
can read your signs, lead you toward freedom.

Published in Poetry Society of Michigan Anthology, *2023*

POEMS BY EDITORS

SUKRITA
Blue Islets

blue

      of the sky
          of the Mediterranean

of my bottomless heart

*

light flowing outward
transiting between goals

darkness descending
inward

*

darkness swallowing
all shadows
left behind by the sun

the moon
beckons them back

*

the moon invites
shadows inside my being

the sun gulps darkness
inviting shadows
outside my self

*

what makes me say
this pen in my fingers
is mine, directed by me

the pen makes a poem
in my diary
on its own

*

when I run
to catch
my own shadow

i catch the full moon
over my head

*

the solid Prussian blue
lying still on the surface
of the ocean

is see-through

melts as I dive into it

Published in Salt & Pepper, *Poetrywala, 2023*

VINITA AGRAWAL
Stroke

A morning might begin like this, windows closing to light,
a punch of darkness delivered to the solar plexusof a day.

Your voice barely audible on the phone saying you'd had a fall
that you could barely move, could barely swallow.

I 'll be right there. The long, tight grip of rain
on my heart. Six hours of thinking the worst before I reach.

Kind neighbours have shifted you to the hospital. You're in the
ICU, tubes and wires rudely in and out of your body.

I climb the mountain of the moment. Your eyes brighten when they
spot me. Your gaze sews my fears. Daddy. Our hands cling.

Tomorrow I'll know a numbness colder than your skin.
A flatteningof all things. How will I vocalise the rising rale of pain?

Loss, a Peepul tree, will take roots inside my chest.
For years it will grow – leaf by leaf. For years the earth will feel heavier.

Published in Mingled Voices 7, *April 2023 Proverse, Hongkong*

BEACON LIGHT

BIBHU PADHI

Bibhu Padhi has published eighteen full-length collections of poetry. His poems have appeared in major magazines throughout the English-speaking world, such as *Contemporary Review*, *New Humanist*, *London Magazine*, *Poetry Review*, *Times Literary Supplement*, *Poetry Ireland Review*, *Illustrated Weekly of India*, and *Indian Literature*. They have been included in numerous anthologies and high-school/university textbooks, five of the most recent being *Language for a New Century: An Anthology of Poems* (New York: Norton), *Journeys* (London: HarperCollins), *The HarperCollins Book of English Poetry*. He lives with his family in Bhubaneswar, India.

Another Need

You've spent your years
asking for nothing, and when
someone told you, you'd

never get anything without
asking for it, you said,
"That's not my business.

The days and nights should know
better, must respond to my needs.
In your instances, you included

the earth's quiet rotation round
the sun, a sapling's slow

rise through space and time".

You should know that they'd
asked for it time and again.
Asking is giving, no less, no more.

"I'd not ask for anything", you said.
You said, "I've been given more
than enough, I never asked for it".

You said, "You may not know, but
silences have their own modes of prayer
just as words do, but different, less

less visible, perhaps less conceited. I can't
ask for things even in silence. Words left me
one night long ago. I never asked for it."

Published in The Awakenings Review, *USA, Spring-2023 Issue*

SHRADDHANJALI

KEKI N. DARUWALLA
(24-01-1937 - 26-09-2024)

Keki Nasserwanji Daruwalla was an Indian poet and short story writer in English. He was also a Indian Police Service officer. His first book of poetry was *Under Orion,* which was published by Writers Workshop, India, in 1970. He then went on to publish his second collection *Apparition in April* in 1971 for which he was given the Uttar Pradesh State Award in 1972. He received the Commonwealth Poetry Prize for Asia in 1987. He was awarded the Sahitya Akademi Award, in 1984 for his poetry collection, *The Keeper of the Dead*. He returned the same award in October 2015 in protest against the use of physical violence against authors. He had 12 volumes of poetry and three novels, the latest being *"Swerving to Solitude"* Simon And Schuster. He wrote a political column for the Tribune.

Of Ledges and Moss

You don't have to notice a gun
to visualise black buck falling
in a fusillade of hoofs.

And the bellies of wild geese
flying in formation?
What is there to visualise

I hear a gunshot
though I don't see a gun.
I don't even hear the shot—
its all in the mind.
It will spin as it falls
huddling into its wings.

Just because I haven't
pulled out a pad of moss
from some rocky ledge,
doesn't mean I do not hear
the rip and tear of rending.
Just because I do not shoot
quail or partridge it doesn't mean
this birdlessness travelling towards me
like a visible void,
does not smother me.
Nature's empire is not confined
to forest and savannah.
The soul is also one of its habitats

COMMEMORATION

Nissim Ezekiel Birth Centenary
(born 1924)

Nissim Ezekiel (1924-2004), known as the Father of Modern Indian Poetry in English, was a foundational figure in postcolonial Indian Writing in English. He was born in a Bene Israel Indian Jewish family in Bombay. He wore many hats: poet, editor, art critic, playwright, and professor of English and American Literature at the University of Bombay. Poetry was always front and center of his life, and he tirelessly mentored many young poets, placing much emphasis on the craft of poetry. He received the Sahitya Akademi award in 1983 and the Padma Shri in 1988. His Birth Centenary year starts on 16 December 2024.

The Second Candle

What's the second candle for, I asked
my wife that Friday night. Wait, she said,
till they are lit and the prayer is over.
Then she turned to me with a cunning smile.
The first candle is for God's daily blessings,
just the usual things, you know,
Life itself, food and drink, love, children,
friends, relatives, books, flowers,
freedom from misfortunes,
all the plain prose of daily breath
which, for me, is poetry, she paused,
wanting me to repeat the question
What's the second candle for?
I didn't repeat it, patiently silent…
Then she added quickly before turning away,
The second candle is for a miracle I need
a special favor, a certain turn of events
what work alone will never bring,
a gift we do not quite deserve
but still may get by asking for it.
Call it grace, if you like, a windfall,
bonus, dearness allowance,
more than a promotion,
Some kind of new dimension, revelation
Well, that's what the second candle's for.
Now do you understand.
She didn't wait for my answer.
I looked at the two candles shining there
and wondered at the faith
that deals so simply with its God.

The poem in Nissim Ezekiel's own handwriting.

The Second Candle

What's the second candle for, I asked
my wife that Friday night. Wait, she said,
till they are lit and the prayer is over.
Then she turned to me with a cunning smile.
The first candle is for God's daily blessings,
just the usual things, you know,
Life itself, food and drink, love, children,
friends, relatives, books, flowers,
freedom from misfortunes,
all the plain prose of daily breath
which, for me, is poetry. She paused,
wanting me to repeat the question.
What's the second candle for?
I didn't repeat it, patiently silent...
Then she added quietly before turning away,
The second candle is for a miracle I need
a special favour, a certain turn of events
what work alone will never bring.
a gift we do not quite deserve
but still may get by asking for it.
Call it grace, if you like, a windfall,
bonus, dearness allowance,
more than a promotion,
some kind of new dimension, revelation.
Well, that's what the second candle's for.
Now do you understand.

She didn't wait for my answer.
I looked at the two candles shining there
and wondered at the faith
that deals so simply with its God.

BIOS

1.   **Abhishek Anicca** is a writer, poet and performance artist based in Patna, India. He is the writer of *The Grammar of My Body* (Penguin Random House India, 2023), a collection of memoir essays on living with disability and chronic illness.

2.   **Aditi Garg** is a journalist by education and a senior copywriter by profession. She has contributed dozens of cover stories, articles and book reviews to national dailies over 25 years. Her work has appeared in *Hakara, Gulmohur Quarterly, Verse of Silence, From My Window, In Parentheses* and *Cool Beans Lit.*

3.   **Aftab Yusuf Shaikh**'s English, Urdu and Hindi poetry has been published in various journals and anthologies. He has published a novel *The Library Girl* (2017), a children's book *Letters to Ammi* (2019) and three volumes of poetry *Tehzeeb Talkies* (2019), *Mominpura* (2021) and *Ansari's Daughter* (2024).

4.   **Ajay Kumar** is the author of *balancing acts* (Yavanika Press, 2022). His poems have appeared in *Usawa, The Bombay Literary Magazine, The Bangalore Review, gulmohur, nether,* and *The Yearbook of Indian Poetry in English 2021,* among others. He lives and studies in Hyderabad.

5.   **Akshada Shrotriya** is a graduate in English literature from Miranda House, and profoundly loses herself in literature and art. In March 2023, she was selected for the Kolam Writers' Workshop. Her works have found home in *Muse India, ASAP Art, Punch Magazine, Borderless Journal, Gulmohur Quarterly,* among others.

6.   **Amit Shankar Saha** is the author of six books including three collections of poems: *Balconies of Time, Fugitive Words*, and *Illicit Poems*. He has won the Wordweavers Prize and has been nominated for the Pushcart Prize, the Griffin Poetry Prize and the Best of Net anthology.

7.   **Amlanjyoti Goswami** has written two books of poetry, *River Wedding* and *Vital Signs*. *River Wedding* was shortlisted for the Sahitya Akademi award. Published around the world, including in *Poetry, The Poetry Review* and *Penguin Vintage*, he is a Best of the Net and Pushcart nominee. He grew up in Guwahati and lives in Delhi.

8.   **Anannya Nath** is an Assistant Professor of English based in Assam. Her short stories, poems and translations have appeared in *Muse India, Monograph, Rhodora, Gulmohur Quarterly*, etc. She was longlisted for the Mozhi Prize, 2023 for translating Lakshminath Bezbaroah's Assamese story, "Madhoimaloti" into English.

9.   **Anil Petwal** is a civil servant with the Government Of Uttarakhand and a writer. His writing has appeared in *Outlook, The Yearbook Of Indian Poetry 2022, The Hooghly Review, The Punch Magazine,The Provenance Journal, Lavender Lime Literary, The Ayaskala* among other places. He can be reached on X on @IamAnilpetwal.

10.   **Anju Kishore**, formerly a finance professional, is a Pushcart Prize 2022 nominee, a published poet, and an award-winning editor of numerous free-verse anthologies. Her book of poems, '*...and I Stop to Listen*' was well received. Her poems, some of them prize-winning have been part of many anthologies and journals

11.   **Anushri Nanavati** is the author of *Birds, Bones, & Melancholia: Musings and Mutterings* and the founder of Haiku & Hymns Creativity Classes for Children in Ahmedabad, India, where she teaches creative writing, literature, psychology, history, and foreign languages.

12.   **Arjun Rajendran**'s latest book is One Man Two Executions (*Westland/Pratilipi 2020*). He is the founder of the poetry community, *The Quarantine Train*. Arjun has recently appeared in some of these anthologies: *The Penguin Book of Indian Poets*, *The Gollancz Book of Indian Science Fiction*, and *Eclectica Magazine: Best Poetry*.

13.   **Arun Paria** lives in Pune. His poems have been published in *The Bombay Literary Magazine*, *nether Quarterly*, *Shiuli*, *Madras Courier*, *Poetry India*, *Heartwood Literary Magazine*, *Anthropocene*, *Yearbook of Indian Poetry 2021*, *Outlook*, and *Indian Literature*. He founded the Pune Writers' Group, a creative community serving over 2000 writers.

14.   **Athira Unni** is a researcher and poetess living in Leeds, UK. Her debut poetry collection *Gaea and Other Poems* (2020) was published by Writer's Workshop, Kolkata. Her poems have appeared in *Channel magazine*, *New Note Poetry*, *Gulmohar Quarterly*, *Paper Dragon*, *The Alipore Post*, etc. She is fascinated by octopuses.

15.   **Atreyee Majumder** is an anthropologist and poet based in Bangalore. The first collection of her poems *The Book of Blue* is out in 2024 from Red River.

16.   **Babitha Marina Justin** is an academic, poet and artist. Her poems, short stories and articles have appeared in various journals.

17.   **Barnali Ray Shukla** is a filmmaker and a published poet. Her poetry, creative writing, essays have been published in India, UK, USA, Australia, Singapore, China, Japan and Hong Kong. Some of her poetry has been translated to Mandarin & Japanese. Her book of poems, *Apostrophe* (RLFPA 2017) is her first book of poems.

18.   **Basudhara Roy** teaches English at Karim City College affiliated to Kolhan University, Chaibasa. Drawn to themes of gender and ecology, her four published books include three collections of poems. A firm believer in the therapeutic power of verse, she writes, reviews,

and sporadically curates and translates poetry from Jamshedpur, Jharkhand.

19.   **Beni Sumer Yanthan** is the pen name of YanbeniYanthan. She is a writer and academic from Nagaland. Her works encompassing poetry, essays, reviews and short stories have been published in various journals, e-zines, newspapers and forums. She is currently Assistant Professor at Nagaland University, Kohima.

20.   **Bhaswati Ghosh** writes and translates fiction, non-fiction and poetry. Her first book of fiction is *Victory Colony, 1950*. Her first work of translation from Bengali into English is *My Days with RamkinkarBaij*. Bhaswati's writing has appeared in several literary journals. She lives in Ontario, Canada.

21.   **Binu Karunakaran** is a poet, translator and journalist based in Kochi, Kerala. A winner of Charles Wallace India Trust Fellowship, his portfolio of poems *Muchiri*, was commended by the Michael Marks Awards for Poetry Pamphlets 2021 judged by panel headed by UK's poet laureate Ruth Padel.

22.   **Carol D'Souza** is a writer and translator from Bangalore.

23.   **Chaitali Sengupta** is a writer and translator. Her debut collection of prose poems *Cross Stitched Words*, won the 'Honorable Mention' (New England Book Festival 2021). Her translation work *Timeless Tales in Translation*, won the Special Jury award in the PILF in 2022. *The Crossings* is her new book of poems.

24.   **C.P. Surendran** is a poet, novelist, and screenplay writer. His collected poems is *Available Light* and his latest novel is *One Love And The Many Lives of Osip B.* He divides his time between Delhi and Kerala and, often, in places in between.

25.   **Debmalya** (he/him) is a writer and mathematician. His poems, essays and translations have appeared or are forthcoming in *The Bangalore Review, Propel, Anthropocene Poetry, The Hooghly Review,*

CounterClock and *Spacebar*, among other literary journals. He has lived by the rivers Ganga, Kaveri, Teesta, Rhea and Thames.

26. **Deepa Agarwal** is an author and poet with over 60 books for children and adults. Her awards include the NCERT National Award for Children's Literature among others. Apart from several contributions in journals and anthologies, she has published two collections of poetry—*Do Not Weep Lonely Mirror* and *Forgotten Kaleidoscopes.*

27. **Devashish Makhija** is a widely published Indian author, graphic artist, poet and filmmaker. His oeuvre includes the award-winning YA novel *Oonga,* the collection of short stories *Forgetting,* graphic-verse collection *OccupyingSilence,* several picture books for children, the award-winning feature films *Joram, Bhonsle, Ajji,* and several acclaimed short films.

28. **Dipanjali Roy** is a poet from Gurgaon, India. She is a recipient of the Queen Mary Wasafiri New Writing Prize in Poetry and has placed at the Rialto Nature & Place Poetry Competition, among others. Her recent work appears in *Gutter Magazine, Wildness, Prototype, The Rialto, LUMIN, nether Quarterly,* and *Wasafiri.*

29. **Durga Prasad Panda** is an accomplished bilingual poet and critic whose works have appeared in prestigious journals across the country and abroad; own Indian Literature Translation Prize from Sahitya Akademi; attended World Congress of Poets in 2019; edited a 'Reader' on the life and works of eminent poet Jayanta Mahapatra.

30. **Feby Joseph** is a part-time flâneur, and full-time piano teacher from Mumbai. He is the winner of Reuel International Poetry Prize, 2020. Some of his works have appeared in *Zoetic Press, The Bangalore Review* and *The Bombay Literary Magazine.*

31. **Gauri Awasthi** from Kanpur has won fellowships from *Yaddo, Sundress Academy for The Arts, Hambidge Cente*r, *Hedgebrook,* and

others. Her writing has been published in *Quarterly West, Notre Dame Review, The Rumpus, Buzzfeed* and others. She is an Associate Editor at *The Offing* and teaches the Decolonizing Poetry Workshop.

32.   **Gayatri Lakhiani Chawla** is an award-winning poet, translator, healer and French teacher from Mumbai. She is the author of three poetry collections – *Borders and Broken Hearts, Invisible Eye, The Empress*. She is the author of *Healing Elixir: The Hawakal Handbook of Angel Therapy, Numerology & Remedies.*

33.   **Geetha Ravichandran** is a retired IRS officer. She writes a monthly column for *The New Indian Express*. Her poetry has appeared in several journals and anthologies. She has written two books of poetry, *Arjavam* and *The Spell of the Rain Tree* published by Red River. She lives in Chennai.

34.   **Gopal Lahiri** is a bilingual poet, critic, editor, writer and translator with 29 books published, including eight jointly edited books. His poetry is published across more than 100 anthologies/journals globally and is translated into 18 languages. He is the first recipient of Jayanta Mahapatra National Award for Literature, 2024.

35.   **Gopikrishnan Kottoor**is a familiar voice in Indian Poetry in English. He has won major awards for his poetry and has been extensively anthologized.

36.   **Huzaifa Pandit** teaches English Literature. He writes poetry in English and translates poetry from Urdu and Kashmiri. Some of his works have found home in magazines like *PaperCuts, Outlook* and *Poetry at Sangam*. His only book of poems – *Green is the Colour of Memory* was published in 2018.

37.   **Imtiaz Dharker** was awarded the Queen's Gold Medal for Poetry in 2014, the Cholmondeley Award in 2010 and Chancellorship of Newcastle University in 2020. Her seven collections include *Over*

the Moon and the latest, *Shadow Reader*. Her poems have featured on BBC radio, television, and the London underground.

38.   **Inam Hussain Begg Mullick** is an award-winning Kolkatan poet. His collections of poems include *Roses for the Madhouse*, *Winter's Electric Architecture* and *The Magical Life of Inamorato*. He has edited the anthologies *Peacocks In a Dream*, *Freedom Raga 2020*, *The Kolkata Cadence* and *The Violet Sun* (forthcoming).

39.   **Indu Parvathi**(she/her) is a poet from Bengaluru, India. Her poetry appears in various literary magazines and platforms including publications in The Yearbook of Indian Poetry 2021& 2022, nether quarterly, Usawa Literary Review, Nightingale& Sparrow, Eunoia Review, The Seventh Wave Magazine, Eclectica Magazine & Kitaab Quarterly.

40.   **Irwin Allan Sealy** is the author of *The Trotter-Nama* and other novels. His Zelaldinus is a cycle of Fatehpur Sikri poems. He has also written the travel books *Yukon to Yucatan* and the *China Sketchbook*, and a memoir, *The Small Wild Goose Pagoda*, set in his hometown, Dehra Dun.

41.   **Jim Wungramyao Kasom** is a photographer, and author. Born and raised in a village in Manipur, Jim has lived in cities for most of his life and dreams of reuniting with his homeland. Writing about home is a self-indulging therapy to cope with the space and time away from home.

42.   **Johannes Manjrekar** (1957-2020) taught at the Maharaja Sayajirao University, Baroda. He pursued other interests including photography and translation, satirical pieces on contemporary life and politics, and haikus, for which he came to be known by the community of poets. *Jacarandas are a Deep Shade of Blue* was published posthumously.

43.   **Jonaki Ray** is an award-winning poet, writer, and editor. Her work has been published in *Poetry*, *Poetry Wales*, *The Rumpus*, *Lunch Ticket*, *Indian Literature*, and elsewhere. She is the author of *Firefly Memories* (Copper Coin, India) and *Lessons in Bending* (Sundress Publications, USA).

44.   **Jyotirmoy Sil** is a dilettante poet. Presently he is an Assistant Professor of English at Malda College, West Bengal. Some of his English poems have been published in *Muse India*, *Madras Courier*, *Spillwords*, *International Times*, *Setu: A Bilingual Magazine*, *Yearbook of Indian Poetry in English 2021*, among others.

45.   **K. Srilata** is a poet, fiction writer, translator and academic. Her most recent collection of poems *Three Women in a Single-Room House* was published by Sahitya Akademi in 2023. Srilata's other books include five collections of poetry.

46.   **Kabir Deb** is a poet/book reviewer hailing from Karimganj, Assam. He has received three international awards for his books. He runs a mental health library. His works have been published in *Sahitya Akademi*, *Outlook*, *Financial Express* and other magazines. He edits interviews for *Usawa Literary Review*.

47.   **Kandala Singh** is a writer from New Delhi living in Pittsburgh. She has received a Dietrich Fellowship from the University of Pittsburgh, and a 2023 Katherine Bakeless Contributor Award in Poetry from the Bread Loaf Writers' Conference. Her poems appear in *Rattle*, *Eclectica*, and elsewhere.

48.   **Kashiana Singh** calls herself a work practitioner and embodies the essence of her TEDx talk - Work as Worship into her every day. She serves as a Managing Editor for *Poets Reading the News*. Her newest collection *Witching Hour* is due to be released in 2024 with Glass Lyre Press.

49.   **Kavita Ezekiel Mendonca** has authored two poetry collections, *'Family Sunday and other poems'*, and *'Light of the Sabbath.'* Her poems have appeared in several anthologies and online journals. She also writes book reviews and Nonfiction. She is the daughter of the late poet, Nissim Ezekiel.

50.   **Kinjal Sethia** is a writer based in Pune. Her work has been published in *nether Quarterly, Usawa Literary Review, EKL Review, Samyukta Fiction* among other places. She is the Associate Editor for Fiction at *The Bombay Literary Magazine (TBLM)*.

51.   **Kinshuk Gupta** is a doctor, bilingual writer, poet and columnist who works at the intersection of gender, health and sexuality. His debut book of short fiction, *Yeh Dil Hai Ki Chordarwaja*, modern Hindi's first LGBT short story collection, was published to great critical acclaim in 2023.

52.   **Kiriti Sengupta**, the 2018 Rabindranath Tagore Literary Prize recipient, has poems published in *The Common, The Florida Review Online, Headway Quarterly,* and elsewhere. He has authored twelve books of poetry and prose; two books of translation; and edited eight anthologies. Sengupta is the chief editor of *Ethos Literary Journal*.

53.   **Lina Krishnan** is an abstract artist and poet in Auroville. *Lemon Vipassana* was published in the *RIC Journal, Dull as Ditchwater* in *Count Every Breath, A Breezy Day* in *Soul Spaces: Poems on Cities, Towns, and Villages*. Lina has a chapbook of nature verse with the Blank Rune Press, Melbourne.

54.   **Madhu Raghavendra** has authored four books of poetry. He collaborates with global artists to create cross disciplinary poetry experiences. He is an IWP fellow at the University of Iowa, and a Charles Wallace Writing Fellow at the University of Stirling. He curates the multidisciplinary Ajanta Ellora Arts Residency.

55. **Malashri Lal**, Professor, Department of English (retd.) University of Delhi, has published 21 books including the 'Goddess trilogy' (co-edited with Namita Gokhale), *In Search of Sita, Finding Radha*, and *Treasures of Lakshmi*. Lal recently published *Mandalas of Time: Poems*. Her poetry has appeared in anthologies and online portals, globally.

56. **Mamang Dai** is a poet and novelist from Pasighat, Arunachal Pradesh. A former journalist, Dai worked with World Wide Fund for nature in the Eastern Himalaya Biodiversity Hotspots programme. His first publication *Arunachal Pradesh: The Hidden Land* (Non-fiction) received the state Verrier Elwin Award. He is a Padma Shri awardee.

57. **Mandakini Bhattacherya** is Associate Professor of English, poet, literary critic and translator, with her own Poetry Page on the Dallas-based *Mad Swirl Magazine*. A participant in the Sahitya Akademi's All India Young Writers' Meet in 2020, she co-translated *A Life Uprooted: A Bengali Dalit Refugee Remembers*.

58. **Mani Rao** is the author of books of poetry including *Sing to Me* (Recent Work Press 2019) and books in translation including *Bhagavad Gita* (HarperCollins 2023) and *Saundarya Lahiri* (Harpercollins 2022), and an academic book called *Living Mantra: Mantra, Deity and Visionary Experience Today* (Palgrave Macmillan 2019).

59. **Meena Chopra**, a Canadian-Indian poet, author, visual artist, and curator of art and literary events, has seen her poetry featured in numerous magazines and anthologies. She champions the fusion of literature with various art forms, boasting a track record of successful collaborations in this innovative realm.

60. **Meenakshi Mohan** is an academic writer, poet, and artist. Her most recent books are *The Rebirth of the Demon* and *Tapestry of Women in Indian Mythology*. Meenakshi is on the Editorial Board of

Inquiry in Education, a peer-reviewed journal of National Louis University, Chicago. Meenakshi lives in Potomac, Maryland.

61.   **Menka Shivdasani** is an award-winning poet, editor and translator with four poetry collections. Her works include an anthology of Sindhi Partition poetry as co-translator, two anthologies for *bigbridge.org* as editor and four collections of poetry. Menka is co-Chair, Asia Pacific Writers and Translators.

62.   **Mrinalini Harchandrai**'s poetry and fiction have placed in several international prizes including the Quarterly West Poetry Prize, Commonwealth Short Story Prize and Columbia Journal Spring Contest, among others. Her novel, *Rescuing A River Breeze* (Bloomsbury, 2023) longlisted for the McKitterick Prize 2021 and The Asian Prize for Fiction 2024.

63.   **Mugdha Sinha** dabbles in poetry when not writing *sarkari* note sheets. *Postcard Poems* is her debut collection of epigrammatic poems sprinkled with wit and wisdom. A career civil servant posted as Joint Secretary (GLAM) in the Ministry of Culture, she is currently working on her next collection titled *Gatherings*.

64.   **Mustansir Dalvi**'s books of poems are *brouhahas of cocks*, *Cosmopolitician* and *Walk*. His poems have been translated into French, Croatian, Marathi, Hindi and Gujarati. His latest book is a translation of Hemant Divate's *Paranoia*, winner of the Maharashtra State Kavi Keshavsut Award from Marathi.

65.   **N. Sehar** is a poet, copywriter, and design student. Her work has appeared in *Gulmohur Quarterly* ,*The Hooghly Review, Broken Antler Magazine, LiveWire, The Alipore Post, and Remington Review* among others. She loves to read about cultures, folklore, and anything that lies at the intersection of art and tech.

66.   **Namrata Pathak** is an academic, critic and writer. She has been a recipient of FCT-Ford Foundation Fellowship and UGC-

Associateship by IIAS, Shimla. She has five books to her credit and three are upcoming from reputed publishers. She was a Charles Wallace India Trust Fellow at SOAS-University of London, 2022-2023.

67. **Namratha Varadharajan** writes to explore emotions, relationships, and nature while trying to chip at the prejudices that plague us, one syllable at a time. Her work has been published in *Briefly Write, Muse India, Usawa Literary Review, The Yearbook of Indian Poetry 2021, The Gulmohar Quarterly, Kali Project*, among others.

68. **Neha R. Krishna**, a Mumbai-based poet and translator, has translated Gulzar's *Triveni* into English tanka. She is also the author of *No Urgency to Be Home*, a collection of haiku and tanka.

69. **Nikita Parik** is the Charles Wallace Fellow at the University of Stirling. Her book *My City is a Murder of Crows* is a Sahitya Akademi Yuva Puraskar & Rabindranath Tagore Literary Prize nominee. She has held talks, readings, and workshops at SOAS University of London, University of Kent, & University of Stirling.

70. **Nishi Chawla** is an academician and a writer. She has seven collections of poetry, nine plays, four feature films, and two novels, to her credit. She has also co-edited two global poetry anthologies of poems published by Penguin Random House, India.

71. **Oindri Sengupta** is a teacher of English in a Govt school. Her poetry has appeared in *The Lake, Tint Journal, Amethyst Review, Outlook India, International Women's Writing Guild, Abridged, Plato's Caves Online, Dreich Magazine, Yearbook Of Indian Poetry in English 2022*, and are upcoming in *Suspect Journal* (Singapore Unbound Press).

72. **Pervin Saket** is a poet, novelist and editor. She received the Srinivas Rayaprol Poetry Prize 2021, and she was the inaugural Fellow for the Vancouver Manuscript Intensive, 2021. She is the Literature

curator of the Kala Ghoda Arts Festival. Her most recent series includes ten biographies on pioneering Indian women.

73.   **Prabhu S. Guptara** has found his poems accepted for publication since the 1960s. He edited *An Anthology of Contemporary Indian Religious Poetry in English* and *Selected Poems of Leela Dharmaraj*. In 2017, Skylark Publications, UK, chose him Poet of the Month. He is included in Debrett's *People of Today*.

74.   **Pramila Venkateswaran**, poet laureate of Suffolk County, Long Island (2013-15) and co-director of Matwaala: South Asian Diaspora Poetry Festival, is the author of many poetry volumes, the most recent being *We Are Not a Museum* (Finishing Line Press, 2022), winner of New York Book Festival award.

75.   **Priya Sarukkai Chabria** is poet, translator and writer. She has edited two poetry anthologies. Winner, Muse India Translation Prize, Kitaab Experimental Story Award, Best Reads from Feminist Press. Awarded for Outstanding Contribution to Literature. On Advisory Councils of G100 India and WrICE, Australia, Founding Editor, *Poetry at Sangam*.

76.   **Priyanka Sacheti** is a writer and poet based in Bangalore, India. She's written about art and culture for many international digital and print publications. Her literary work and art have appeared in journals such as *Barren, Common, The Selkie, The Lunchticket*, and *Sunlight Press* along with past and forthcoming anthologies.

77.   **R. Suresh Babu** hails from Thiruvalla in Kerala. His haiku was shortlisted for the Touchstone Awards for Individual Poems in 2022. He is the winner of the World Online Kukai, Kyoto Haiku Project 2021 and received an Honorable mention in the 75th Bashō Memorial English Haiku Contest, 2021.

78.   **Radha Chakravarty** is a poet, critic and translator. *Subliminal* is her debut collection of poetry. Her poems have appeared in

numerous journals and anthologies. She has published over 20 books, including translations of major Bengali writers. She contributed to "Pandemic: A Worldwide Community Poem", nominated for the Pushcart Prize 2020.

79.   **Rahana K. Ismail** is the author of 'Newtness' (Yavanika Press, 2022). Her poems have been featured in *The Yearbook of Indian Poetry in English (2021, 2022)*, *Penn Review, Usawa Literary Review, POSIT, Alchemy Spoon, nether Quarterly, Muse India, Aainanagar, Setu, Aleph Review, Contemporary Haibun Online, Last Leaves,* among others.

80.   **Ramesh Karthik Nayak** is a Banjara writer, who writes in the Banjara dialect through the Telugu script and in Telugu and English. He is one of the first writers to depict the Banjara lifestyle in literature. He was thrice shortlisted for the Sahitya Akademi Yuva Puraskar in Telugu.

81.   **Ranjit Hoskote**'s collections of poetry include *Central Time, Jonahwhale, Hunchprose* and *Icelight.* Hoskote is the author of the acclaimed translation, *I, Lalla: The Poems of Lal Ded* and a book of essays on Gieve Patel, *To Break and To Branch.*

82.   **Ranu Uniyal** is Professor English at University of Lucknow, and founding member of PYSSUM, an organization for people with special needs. Her poetry books include *Across the divide* (2006), *December poems* (2012) and *The Day We Went Strawberry Picking In Scarborough* (2018), (Hindi) *Saeeda Ke Ghar* 2021.

83.   **Reshma Ruia** has published two novels, *Something Black in the Lentil Soup* and *Still Lives,* winner of the 2023 Diverse Book Readers' Choice Award, a poetry collection, *A Dinner Party in the Home Counties,* 2019 Word Masala Award winner and a short story collection, *Mrs Pinto Drives to Happiness.*

84.   **Rhitama Basak** is a research scholar of Comparative Literature. She has majored in the discipline at Jadavpur University

Kolkata, UBB, Romania and University of Delhi. She has been a recipient of the Erasmus+ scholarship and RUSA research and travel grant. She is working on Sufi reception in Progressive Urdu poetry.

85.   **Rishi Dastidar**'s third collection, *Neptune's Projects*, is published in the UK by Nine Arches Press. He is editor of *The Craft: A Guide to Making Poetry Happen in the 21st Century* (Nine Arches Press), and co-editor of *Too Young, Too Loud, Too Different: Poems from Malika's Poetry Kitchen* (Corsair).

86.   **Rochelle Potkar** is Novelist, Poet, Screenwriter and author of *Paper Asylum* (haibun) – shortlisted for the Rabindranath Tagore Literary Prize 2020; *Four Degrees of Separation* (free verse); *Bombay Hangovers* (short fiction); and *Coins in Rivers* (upcoming poetry book), an alumna of Iowa's International Writing Program, and a Charles Wallace Fellow at the University of Stirling.

87.   **Ruth Vanita** has published two collections of verse, two novels (*Memory of Light*, 2023; *A Slight Angle*, 2024), and several other books, including *Love's Rite: Same-Sex Marriages in Modern India*. She has translated many works from Hindi and Urdu to English, most recently Mahadevi Varma's *My Family*.

88.   **Sahana Ahmed** is a poet and novelist based in Gurugram, India. She is the author of *Combat Skirts* (2018) and the editor of *Amity: peace poems* (2022).

89.   **Saima Afreen** is a poet, essayist, journalist, and teaching-artist. She authored poetry collection *Sin of Semantics* and a chapbook *Winter Biomythography*. Her works have been published across Europe, North America, South Asia, and Australia. She was Charles Wallace Fellow for Creative Writing at the University of Kent, U.K. (2019).

90.   **Sambhu R** is a bilingual poet from Kerala. He is employed as Assistant Professor of English at N.S.S. College, Pandalam. His poems

in English have appeared in *Wild Court, Bombay Literary Journal, Muse India, Borderless Journal, Setu* and *Shot Glass Journal,* among others.

91.   **Sangita Kalarickal** is a Pushcart Prize and Touchstone award nominated wordsmith. Her work is widely published in several journals and anthologies. Her first chapbook of poems is *Mamina (Kavya-Adisakrit, 2023).* She is an associate editor of *Drifting Sands Haibun Journal* and conducts the podcast *Ripples in the Sand.*

92.   **Sanjeev Sethi** has authored seven books of poetry. He has been published in over thirty countries. In 2023, he won the first prize in a poetry competition at the prestigious *National Defence Academy,* Pune. He was recently conferred the 2023 Setu Award for Excellence. He lives in Mumbai.

93.   **Sanjukta Das gupta** is a poet, short story writer, critic and translator. She was a member of the General Council of Sahitya Akademi New Delhi and Convenor, English Advisory Board, Sahitya Akademi, New Delhi. She is the President of the Intercultural Poetry and Performance Library, Kolkata.

94.   **Sarabjeet Garcha** is the author of five books of poems. He has received the Fellowship for Outstanding Artists from the Government of India, the International Publishing Fellowship from the British Council, and the inaugural Godyo Podyo Probondho Award. His poems have been translated into several languages.

95.   **Saranya Subramanian** is a poet, writer, and theatre practitioner based in Bombay. An MFA graduate from the University of San Francisco, she has been published in *Lithub, The Caravan, Aainanagar* among others. She runs The Bombay Poetry Crawl, an archival and research space dedicated to the 20th century Bombay Poets.

96.   **Saraswati Nagpal** is an Indian poet, writer of fantasy and sci-fi, and a classical dancer. Her graphic novels are feminist retellings of epic Indian myths. She is published in *The Atlantic, Atlanta Review, Acropolis Journal, Tipton Poetry* & others. Saraswati has a forthcoming chapbook with Black Bough Poetry, Wales.

97.   **Sekhar Banerjee** has been nomination for a Pushcart Award and for a Best of the Net Award. He has been published in *Stand Magazine, Poetry Wales, Indian Literature, Arkana, Ink Sweat and Tears, The Bitter Oleander, The Lake* and elsewhere. He lives in Kolkata, India.

98.   **Shanta Acharya** DPhil (Oxon) is a poet, novelist, writer, and reviewer. The author of twelve books, her publications range from poetry, literary criticism and fiction, to finance. Her latest books of poetry are *Imagine: New and Selected Poems* (HarperCollins, 2017) and *What Survives Is The Singing* (Indigo Dreams, 2020).

99.   **Shantanu Ray Chaudhuri** is either an 'accidental' editor who strayed into publishing from a career in finance and accounts or an 'accidental' finance person who found his calling in publishing. He won the Editor of the Year Award in 2017. He writes on films, music and books.

100.   **Shaurya Pathania** holds a Masters degree in English Literature from University of Delhi. He has a keen interest in poetry. His recent works have been published in *JAKE, A Coup of Owls Press, Vine Leaves Press, Synchronized Chaos* and elsewhere. You can find him @shauryapathani4 on Twitter.

101.   **Shelly Bhoil** has published poetry books in English *An Ember from Her Pyre* (India), Brazilian-Portuguese *Preposição de entendimento* (Brazil) and Spanish *Poemas en construcción* (Colombia). She has edited the reference books *Tibetan Subjectivities on a Global Stage* and *New Narratives of Exile Tibet* for Lexington books. Shelly lives in Brazil.

102. **Shikha Malaviya** is a poet, writer & mentor. Her works include *Anandibai Joshee: A Life in Poems* and *Geography of Tongues*. Her poetry has been nominated for the Pushcart Prize and featured in *Catamaran*, *PLUME*, *Prairie Schooner* & other fine publications.

103. **Shikhandin** is the pen name of an award-winning Indian writer. Books include *The Woman on the Red Oxide Floor* (Red River Story, India), *After Grief – Poems* (Red River, India), *Impetuous Women* (Penguin-RHI), *Immoderate Men* (Speaking Tiger, India), *Vibhuti Cat* (Duckbill-Penguin-RHI) among others. She is widely anthologised and published worldwide.

104. **Shilpa Dikshit Thapliyal** is a *Pushcart Prize, Best of the Net nominee,* andsecond place winner in *The Letter Review Prize. Her poems are in QLRS, PR&TA, Usawa, The Best Asian Poetry-21, Yearbook of Indian Poetry 2020, 2021 and 2022, Shot Glass, Tiger Moth Review, Trivium,* and elsewhere.

105. **Shobhana Kumar** is a poet, translator, chronicler, memoirist and industrial biographer. Her book of haibun, *A Sky Full of Bucket Lists*, won the Rabindranath Tagore Literary Prize and the Touchstone Distinguished Books Award, by The Haiku Foundation. She is a social worker operating in education and branding.

106. **Shruti Sareen** teaches in colleges/universities whenever she manages to find a job. Her poetry collection, *A Witch Like You*, appeared in 2021. She has a fictional memoir on the verge of publication and is engaged in writing speculative fiction, love-letters, and of course, more poetry!

107. **Shyamasri Maji** is a poet and academic. Her debut collection *Forgive Me, Dear Papa and Other Poems* (Hawakal, 2023) has received critical acclaim. Her book reviews, poems and articles have been published in *Kitaab, Indian Literature, Economic & Political Weekly, Asian Review of Books, Café Dissensus* and *Outlook India*.

108. **Siddharth Dasgupta** is a Poet, Fictionist, and Culture Journalist. His most recent book—*All These Streets We've Known By Heart*—was shortlisted for the Rabindranath Tagore Literary Prize and longlisted for the Oxford Bookstore Book Cover Prize. Siddharth is the Visual Narratives Editor with *The Bombay Literary Magazine*.

109. **Sivakami Velliangiri** is included among women poets by Srinivasa Iyengar in *History of Indian Writing in English* (1980). She has an online chapbook *"In My Midriff"* published by *Lily Poetry Review*. Her her debut poetry book is *How We Measured Time*. She is a contributor to *The Penguin Book of Indian Poets*.

110. **Soni Somarajan**'s poetry has featured in *Bombay Literary Magazine, Bangalore Review, Muse India, Madras Courier, Alipore Post, Caesurae;* and in the anthologies: *Open Your Eyes: A Climate Anthology*(2023); *Yearbook of Indian Poetry in English (2020, 2022)*; and *Scent of Rain: Remembering Jayanta Mahapatra (2024). First Contact (2020)* is his debut collection.

111. **Sonnet Mondal** is an Indian poet, editor, and author of *An Afternoon in My Mind, Karmic Chanting, Lautati Dopaharen* and five other books of poetry. Founder director of *Chair Poetry Evenings – Kolkata's International Poetry Festival*, Mondal edits the Indian section of *Lyrikline* and serves as managing editor of *Verseville*. He was a guest editor for *Words Without Borders*, and *Poetry at Sangam*.

112. **Sophia Naz** is a Pushcart Prize nominee, bilingual poet, artist, editor, translator and author of *Bark Archipelago* (Weavers Press, San Francisco & Red River India 2023), *Open Zero* (Yoda Press 2021) *Shehnaz* (Penguin Random House 2019), *Pointillism* (Copper Coin 2017), *Date Palms* (City Press 2017) and *Peripheries* (Cyberhex 2015).

113. **Suchi Govindarajan** is a poet, writer and photographer. She's the author of three picture-books for children. In past lives, she has been a technical writer and a humour columnist. Her work has

appeared in various journals and in anthologies like the *Yearbook of Indian Poetry.*

114. **Sudeep Sen**'s prize-winning books include *Postmarked India: New & Selected Poems, Rain, Aria, The HarperCollins Book of English Poetry, Fractals: New & Selected Poems | Translations 1980-2015, EroText, Kaifi Azmi: Poems | Nazms, Anthropocene,* and *Red.* Sen is the first Asian honoured to speak and read at the Nobel Laureate Festival.

115. **Suhit Bombaywala**'s factual and fictive writings have appeared in the media website and weekend edition of *Hindustan Times;* the anthologies *The Penguin Book of Indian Poets* and *Rivers Going Home,* and literary journals *Guernica, Litro* and *Out of Print.*

116. **Sunil Rajagopal** is a birder, writer and sustainability professional with two published collections of poetry: *"When Ants Grow Wings"*, Authorspress, 2023 and *"What Goes in to a Butterfly"*, Storymirror, 2019. He also writes for publications like *The Hindu, The Businessline, The Wire,* etc.

117. **Sunil Sharma** is a humble word-worshipper, catcher of elusive sounds, meanings, and images with 27 books published. A winner of the **Golden Globe Award-2023, and Nissim Award for Excellence for Prose, 2022,** for *Minotaur,* his poems feature in the **UN project**: *Happiness: The Delight-Tree: An Anthology of Contemporary International Poetry,* 2015.

118. **Tabish Nawaz** teaches Environmental Science and Engineering at IIT Bombay. He has authored a short story collection *Opening Clouds, Fermented Rain (Hawakal, 2020)* and a poetry collection *The Ornaments for Silence (Hawakal, 2023).* He lives in Mumbai

119. **Tansy Troy** is a poet, performer, maker of masks, playwright, educator and editor of young people's journal *The Apple Press.* She shares her work in schools, galleries and theatres across India. You

can read more of her poetry in *Ratnakosha* (Red River, August 2023), and follow her poetic journey @voice_of_the_turtle.

120.   **Taseer Gujral** is a poet, editor, columnist and a translator. Her writings appear in *Coldnoon Diaries, Sahitya Akademi Anthology, Outlook Magazine* and others. She has penned columns for the *DNA*. She has been on the panel for *Kamala Das Award*. Her interests range from culture studies, cinema and aesthetics to music.

121.   **Tasneem Khan** is a writer from Lucknow, India. Her work has appeared in the *Yearbook of Indian Poetry in English 2022, Nether Quarterly, Gulmohur Quarterly, Monograph Magazine, LiveWire, FII* and *The Woman Inc. Magazine*.

122.   **Tejaswinee Roychowdhury** is a Pushcart-nominated writer-poet from India. Her poetry is in *Black Bough, Copihue Poetry, The Bayou Review, Dreich, Paddler Press, The Chakkar*, and more. Her fiction is in *Muse India, Fiery Scribe*, and others. She is the founding editor of *The Hooghly Review* and a lawyer. Twitter: @TejaswineeRC.

123.   **Teji Sethi** is a widely published poet and a haikai disciple. She is the author of *Moss Laden Walls* (2021) and the co-editor of the haiku anthology, *amber I pause* (2023). As the founding editor of *Triya*, a bilingual e-zine, Teji follows a path of art, poetry, and language uniquely.

124.   **Uma Gowrishankar** is a writer and artist from Chennai, South India. Her poems have appeared in online and print journals. Her full-length collection of poetry *Birthing History* was published by Leaky Boot Press.

125.   **Urna Bose** is a writer, poet, editor, and reviewer. She won The Telangana Poetry Forum Enchanting Editor Award, 2019, the Women Empowered Feminine Power Inspiration Award, 2020, and the Nissim International Poetry Prize, 2021. As the Deputy Editor for *Different Truths*, she devotes time to the 'Poet 2 Poet' column there.

126.   **Vidya Shankar**, a widely published writer, Associate Editor for *haiku KATHA Journal*, host for *The Haibun Gallery* and *Spotlight* forums of *Triveni Haikai India*, author of two poetry books, and editor of four anthologies, is an English language teacher in Chennai. She finds meaning to her life through yoga and mandalas.

127.   **Vivek Sharma** has published a book, *The Saga of a Crumpled Piece of Paper* (Writers Workshop, Calcutta, 2009). His work appears in *Atlanta Review, Poetry, The Cortland Review*, and *Muse India*, among others. Vivek is a Pushcart-nominated poet, published scientist, and professor of chemical engineering in Chicago.

128.   **Yamini Dand Shah** is the Assistant Director, Centre for Kachchh at Somaiya Vidyavihar University and Curator at KGAF. She was invited as a writer-in-residence at Tubingen University, Germany and as a research scholar to various Universities in Canada. Author of *Abstract Oralism* and working on it as a literary theory.

129.   **Yuyutsu Sharma** is a recipient of fellowships and grants from The Rockefeller Foundation and Ireland Literature Exchange, "The world-renowned Himalayan poet," (*The Guardian*) and "Himalayan Neruda," Yuyutsu is a vibrant force on the world poetry stage. Punjab-born, Indian poet, he makes his living with poetry.

130.   **Zainab Wahab** is pursuing her Master's in English Literature from Jawaharlal Nehru University. Her poetry has been published in online magazines such as *Monograph* and *Gulmohur Quarterly*. She enjoys writing book reviews, reading Gothic texts and baking for family and friends.

131.   **Zilka Joseph** is an internationally published poet who has authored six collections. Her new book, *Sweet Malida: Memories of a Bene Israel Woman,* explores the history of her community, and her journeys. Among her awards are a Zell Fellowship and the Elsie Lee Scholarship from the University of Michigan.

EDITORS

Sukrita Paul Kumar (born in Kenya) has been a resident poet and Fellow at the International Writing Programme, Iowa. Former Fellow, IIAS (Shimla), and honorary faculty, Durrell Centre, Corfu, she has published many collections of poems and critical works. Currently, Guest Editor, *Indian Literature*, Sahitya Akademi, she held the Aruna Asaf Ali Chair, University of Delhi earlier. The 2023 Tagore Literary Prize was awarded to her for her latest book of selected poems. *Salt and Pepper*.

Vinita Agrawal is the author of six books of poetry. Her book *Twilight Language* won the Proverse Prize, Hongkong in 2021. She has edited two anthologies on climate change, *Open Your Eyes* and *CountEveryBreath*. She won the Tagore Literary Prize in 2018 and the Gayatri GaMarsh Prize, USA, in 2015. She is on the advisory board of the Tagore Literary Prize and co-chair of Global Indian Council of Environment and Sustainability. www.vinitawords.com

ACKNOWLEDGEMENTS

Each year, the *Yearbook of Indian Poetry in English* is primarily an outcome of a collective effort of people who have love for poetry and who wish to help us strengthen the tradition of poetry and its archiving for contemporary readers as well as for posterity. We, the editors, hope to sustain our own energy and commitment to this venture.

A big thank you to our publishers Pippa Rann Books and Media (UK), specifically Prabhu Guptara, for publishing this volume with utmost competence and meticulous care.

Our deeply felt gratitude to each of the members of the committee who worked conscientiously towards selecting quality poems and also maintained the sanctity of anonymous selections. Thank you Imtiaz Dharker, Madhu Raghavendra, Mani Rao, and Vivek Narayanan for being a part of our esteemed Review Committee for the Yearbook 2023. We would also like to sincerely thank Antara Gupta for assisting us.

We are highly obliged to the editors of poetry journals who proactively nominated noteworthy poems for the Yearbook, published in the stipulated year: Amit Saha and Nikita Parik - EKL Review; Anil Menon and Pervin Saket - TBLM; Priya Chabria & Mrinalini Harchandrai - Poetry at Sangam; Semeen Ali - Muse India, and Dibyajyoti Sarma - Red River Press.

Needless to say that the overwhelming number of poets who submitted their poems with faith in this project has been tremendously inspirational. Many thanks dear fellow poets! This is what keeps the Yearbook substantially alive.

And finally the readers. We are grateful that there is an enthusiastic reception of the Yearbook each year. We hope to have more and more readers, scholars, researchers of this literary archive created with such happy labour and love. Thank you all.

Sukrita & Vinita
Editors

PIPPA RANN BOOKS
and
GLOBAL RESILIENCE PUBLISHING
(*imprints of* Salt Desert Media Group Ltd., U.K.)

SALT DESERT MEDIA GROUP LTD. (SDMG), U.K., was established in 2019, and currently publishes under the imprints, Pippa Rann Books and Media (PRBM) and Global Resilience Publishing (GRP).

Pippa Rann Books and Media publishes books about India and the Indian diaspora, for everyone who has an interest in the sub-Continent, it's peoples and cultures. At a time of political challenge, Pippa Rann books aim to nurture the values of democracy, liberty, equality and fraternity that inspired the founders of the modern state of India.

Titles on the Global Resilience Publishing (GRP) list explore how global challenges can be addressed and resolved with an inter-disciplinary and transnational approach. The imprint focuses on subjects such as Climate Change, the Global Financial System, Multilateral and Corporate Governance, etc. In addition to its own publications, Salt Desert Media provides distribution services in English-speaking territories for several authors and publishers.

Sales and Distribution:
- India and SE Asia: Penguin Random House India
- Canada and the USA: Trafalgar Square Press
  (https://www.ipgbook.com/)

- UK: LSS (Sales) Contact: Andrew Wormleighton (andrew@lionsalesservices.com)
- Rest of World/Rights: Prologue Sales
  Contact: Rob Wendover (rob@prologuesales.com)
  Distribution: Marston Book Services above